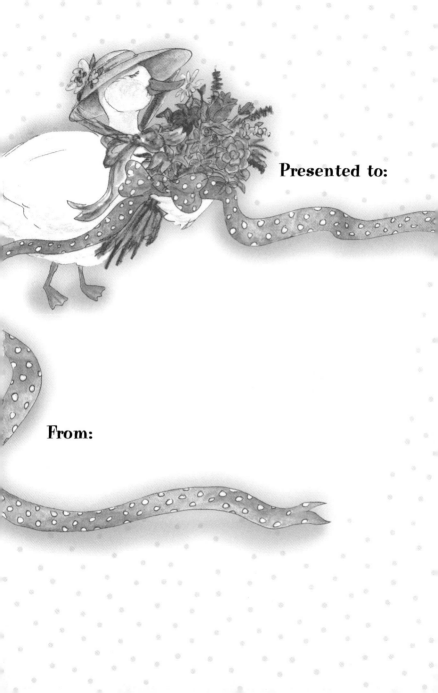

Presented to:

From:

Pull Yourself Up by Your Bra Straps

And Other Quacker Wisdom

★

Pull Yourself Up by Your Bra Straps

And Other Quacker Wisdom

Jeanne Bice

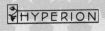

New York

Library of Congress Cataloging-in-Publication Data has been applied for.

Bice, Jeanne.
Pull yourself up by your bra straps : and other quacker wisdom / Jeanne bice.
p. cm
ISBN 1-4013-0235-1
1. Success. 2. Conduct of life. 3. Bice, Jeanne. I. Title

BJ1611.B52 2005

170'.44—dc22   2005050286

Hyperion books are available for special promotions and premiums. For details contact Michael Rentas, Assistant Director, Inventory Operations, Hyperion, 77 West 66th Street, 11th floor, New York, New York 10023, or call 212-456-0133.

FIRST EDITION

10 9 8 7 6 5 4 3 2

To my dear children,
Tim and Lee...

Without you both, this book
would still be a dream. What a team we make!
Did you ever "thunk" it? Thank you, Butchie,
for giving us the courage to go on without you.
We've come so far...
but the best is yet to be!

Contents

Meet the Head Quack

Hi. I'm Jeanne Bice, Head Quack. If you are a Quacker yourself, or simply like to wear my Quacker Factory line of clothing, you already understand what I mean by "Head Quack." If this is the first time you've heard of Quackers, perhaps a little explanation is in order!

Ten years ago, I began selling clothes on QVC. My company, Quacker Factory, produces whimsical designs that help a woman feel better about herself. QVC gave us the perfect venue to show how much fun the clothes are to wear. Happily, women responded to it in a big way.

In the years since then, my life has been enriched in ways I could never have imagined. The most important change has to do with a growing group of women who are not only my customers, but have affectionately started to call themselves "Quackers."

These women came to me to buy clothes, but along the way they have become friends—both to me and to one another. God knows the clothing, which is very embellished and covered in rhinestones, really stands out in a crowd! So when my customers see one another, they instantly form a common bond. They have a reason to go up to one another and say hello—or, more likely, knowing these women, "Quack, quack!"

Yes, we quack at one another. This wasn't intentional. Over the years, people have asked me, "What's the name of your company?" I say, "Quacker Factory. You know, like a duck: 'quack, quack'!"

Soon women from all over started quacking at me. It's a fun way to say hi and break the ice. People used to walk by me and say, "Oh, I know you, you're that lady on QVC." Now they just say, "Quack, quack!" We giggle and laugh and hug, and then we are on our way.

It happens anywhere and everywhere. I love it when I am standing in line at the airport to check in for my flight, along with all the executive-type businessmen of the world, and people keep walking by and quacking at me. After the fifth or sixth person quacks, someone finally has to ask, "What is this quacking all about? Who are you? Are you somebody?"

Of course, my humble Wisconsin upbringing kicks in and I respond, "Oh no, I'm just a funny lady who wears a headband." But truth be known, I am the Head Quack—and hundreds of thousands of women and I have formed a sisterhood. We have a network of friends who all have a common desire to get as much fun out of life on this crazy planet as we can.

Now, I have always had a BIG MOUTH. My husband used to say I was the only woman he knew with calluses on both ankles from putting my foot in my mouth so often. I was born into a family of auctioneers, and they were a loud group who used their ability to talk as a way to make a living. I inherited this gift of gab.

For years I've been telling stories of my life. I've told them on the radio, on QVC, to strangers on the bus . . . and now I'm telling them to you, right in this book.

It is my hope that you are reading this for the joy it will bring you—not as a guidebook, but as a celebration of life, joy, and dreams come true. I'm not asking you to think of me as an authority . . . I come as a friend. I want to share with you some funny, heartwarming stories about my life and the lessons I've spotted along the way. I want to pass along the good things I've learned.

I know your life is full. Each of these stories is just a little snippet—nothing that will take you longer than one trip to the john.

I'm not saying, "Do it my way." It is my hope that this book will inspire you to do it your *own* way. I hope it inspires you to dream, to find your passion, and to go for it with gusto! Find the joy in life! I hope it helps you realize that your dreams are fully within your reach.

Visualize it—dream it—believe it! Reach for the moon; the least that will happen is you will fall among the stars. It doesn't matter whether you are changing jobs, losing weight, finding a new love, surviving a loss, regaining your health, or chasing a dream.

Let these stories encourage you to celebrate the power of your dreams. If I can do it, anyone can. It can happen at the drop of a hat and at any "old" age.

Thanks for sharing the time with me, and I hope you enjoy the thoughts of a fat kid from Fond du Lac, Wisconsin. Now sit down, get a cup of coffee, and let me share with you the lessons I've learned.

What *Is* a Quacker?

A Quacker is . . .

★ Caring
★ Kind
★ Quirky
★ A little bawdy
★ Joyful
★ Slightly bitchy
★ A dreamer
★ A believer
★ All woman!

Pull Yourself Up by Your Bra Straps

1

Playing House

From the time I was four until I was nine, we lived on Fifth Street in Fond du Lac, Wisconsin. Behind our house was a huge barn of a garage that became the neighborhood playground. My dad was an auctioneer. Almost every week he would be on the road calling a household or farm auction. At the end of the day, if there were things that hadn't sold, he would say to the farmer, "I'll give you X number of dollars and clear all this out for you. I'll put it in another auction another time."

Soon our barn was full of furniture of every conceivable size and shape. We had furniture everywhere. On a warm summer day, all of my friends and I would go out to the big old barn, climb up the stairs to the at-

tic, and start pulling stuff down. Soon we would have a kitchen, a living room, a dining room, and a bedroom all set up. Our "house" would have everything that we needed, including an old sink and an even older pump. There was even an old stove we could use. We'd arrange and rearrange all the furniture until it was just right. When we played house, we literally played house!

I grew up during World War II, and in those days you kept all your tin cans and cardboard. My mother stored all our empty cans and empty boxes downstairs in the coal bin off the basement. We'd all troop downstairs to gather stuff for our house. We would carefully set up old oatmeal boxes on the shelves and use the empty cans to fix our meals.

I loved playing house with my friends. It made me feel like a little woman! I think that I learned how to be a housewife from those friends. I'm a Cancer and we are the ultimate nesters. God blessed me with friends who would play house with me. He also blessed me with a father who provided me everything a miniature housewife could need.

I wonder if some of the girls that I played with in those days still like playing house. Have their husbands ever gotten used to their living rooms being constantly rearranged? Do they still look at a room full of furniture as a room full of possibilities? As they push their sofa to the middle of the room for the hundredth time, I wonder if they remember playing house in our big barn behind the old Fifth Street house. I do.

When I got older, I wanted to be a nun. We had moved to Ledgeview Avenue and our house had a huge basement, or rumpus room, where my dad built me a classroom. Once again, his auctions supplied everything I needed to make my dream a reality. The contents of many of the old one-room schoolhouses were being auctioned off as kids moved to the city. Every week he came back from auctions, his truck loaded with blackboards, kids' desks, and even a big teacher desk for me. My mom would give me papers and files from the office so that I could look really busy.

I played nun because I was in Catholic school at the time and knew that I was going to be the greatest teacher God ever put on this earth. I would even dress the part in a long housecoat. I would wrap a feed sack dishtowel around my head and down around my chin. I'd put towel after towel over the top just like the nuns did and then crown the whole thing off with the piano bench cover. I was quite a sight! The whole getup must have weighed forty pounds. Why I am not a humpback today, I don't know.

God gave me a special group of friends and we would play school for hours. I was a really tough teacher because I had the nuns as my role models. I walked the aisles with my ruler and I had my rosary beads hanging from my waist. You know, a friend is someone who thinks you are a good egg, even if you are slightly cracked! Now that I look back on it, my friends may have thought I was slightly cracked, but they played the game anyway. Years later, I became a teacher—but I soon discovered that it was a lot more fun playing in the basement on Ledgeview Avenue with my friends than it was to face an actual classroom.

Childhood friends help us develop our imagination and practice our dreams without fear of criticism. They just play with you and give you a chance to spread your wings. They are never critical and never put the kibosh on your schemes. I am so grateful to all my childhood friends who let me play and dream and develop into who I am today.

No matter what I dreamed, my father provided me with the wherewithal to let my imagination soar. I didn't have to just sit and dream. He helped me put my dream houses together and build my schoolhouses. Who would have guessed that other people's castoffs would be the foundation for me to live out my dreams?

2

Just Ducky

I was a small girl the first time we went to Florida for Christmas vacation. Santa came to my home and left a note saying that our present that year was a trip to Florida. Back in the forties, Florida was not the big deal it is today (there was no Disney World), but all we heard as children was that my father dreamed of moving to Florida and retiring there by 1970. Our whole life was geared toward making this dream a reality. And that year we were off to see his dream place.

On trips my mom always drove. She was much better at it than my dad. It was a forever drive at that time, 2,500 miles of two-lane traffic. My dad spent a lot of the drive in the backseat between my brother and me so we would not fight. He was also our entertainment for the drive. Out of the blue he'd holler, "Stop!" We would all hop out at the place he picked. We'd check out the view from Lookout Mountain in Tennessee, or get an on-the-spot lesson of how sugarcane is grown in Georgia. It was so much fun for two little kids.

After three long days we finally crossed over the border into Florida and the first place Dad hollered to stop at was Cypress Gardens. As we walked through the front gate, there was a huge flock of flamingos . . . oh, but it was magical! If this was what dreaming did for you, then dreaming was good. And yes, he did retire to the Magical Land of Pink Flamingos in 1970.

Dreams really do come true. So, ruffle your little pink feathers and get dreaming!

Liar

Liar, liar, pants on fire . . .

I was a champion liar as a child. Not big lies, just little white ones. Lies to make me popular, lies to keep everyone happy. I was a people pleaser and in my book, pleasing people required little lies. Tiny lies. Also, I was very tender, so I lied to protect my soft side. Now, I never claimed to be a good liar. I just did it often, and I often got caught!

My folks came home one night after working late. They wanted some cheese and crackers, but the Ritz crackers were all gone. My mom asked, "Who ate all the crackers?" My brother immediately started to scream, "I didn't do it, I didn't do it!" My mother said, "Oh, you did it 'cause you doth protest too much." I just kept very quiet and smiled, and he got blamed.

Now, let's look at this seriously, people. I was fat; my brother was very, very skinny. Who do you think ate all the Ritz crackers? But I had learned how to act like the good girl. Poor Dick never learned to be quiet. He always looked guilty. He took a lot of whacks in life because of it, and most were for me, God love him. He turned out normal and still loves me very much to this day. I don't know why, 'cause I smiled while he wailed.

The sad part was that I also lied to myself. I told me that I was not capable of doing anything. I was sweet, but not very bright. I believed me.

What if you are just perfect the way you are? What if there is no need to change, no need to transform yourself into someone thinner, someone more intelligent, more understanding, prettier, funnier, more lovable? Did you ever think you might be perfect, just the way you are?

Love yourself as you are right this moment. Look for all the good about you and love it—love it lots! Once you love where you are and are grateful for all you are, only then can you ask God for some change. Treasure it, see what miracles will happen!

Remember:

Whatever happens . . .
Happens for a reason.
Don't try so hard . . .
the best things come when
you least expect them to.
To the world you may be one person,
but to one person
you may be the world.

I Believe in Quackers!

I believe . . . my Quackers and I could do anything and have a great time.

I believe . . . true Quacker friendships continue to grow, even over long distances.

I believe . . . we Quackers are responsible for what we do, no matter how we feel . . . no crankiness!

I believe . . . no matter how good a Quack friend is, we're going to hurt each other occasionally, and we must forgive.

I believe . . . no matter how bad your heart is broken, a Quack can fix it.

I believe . . . your life can be changed by a Quacker who you don't even know.

I believe . . . that even when we think we have no more to give, if a friend cries out, a Quacker finds the strength to help.

I believe . . . Quackers have learned to play through the small hurts with smiles on their faces.

I believe . . . angels do carry Quackers around by their bra straps.

I believe . . . a Quacker has the heart and soul of someone you would want to be friends with.

I believe . . . my life has been blessed by all the Quackers of the world.

And it is my hope that I have enhanced all of their lives.

Call me Quacky, but I believe I have!

4

Aunt Lena and Uncle Joe

When I was young, we moved from Bell Street to the Fifth Street house where some of my best memories were made. My bestest buddy during that time was my uncle Joe. He and Aunt Lena lived two doors down. Their house was always the perfect place to run when life got too spooky at home or if I ever had a day when I was just plain bored.

My dad's aunt Lena was originally a spinster who worked for rich people and cared for their children. Aunt Lena was as wide as she was tall and a little on the cranky side, but she was also one of the world's best cooks—next to my mom and grandma. Whenever we arrived at her door, she always greeted us with home-made eggnog, insisting that it was healthy for us and would give us energy.

One day, to everyone's surprise, Aunt Lena married a widower who had two small children. Uncle Joe and Aunt Lena were walking proof of the adage that opposites attract. Uncle Joe was a small-framed man who was a carpenter by trade and one of the sweetest people who ever walked the earth. Aunt Lena fed my body while Uncle Joe fed my soul and spirit.

Uncle Joe had great patience as I followed him around like a new puppy, always underfoot. I think a great deal of my creativity comes from hanging around him and watching him work. Time after time I watched as he took the simplest woods and tools and created stunning tables and chairs. He taught me to see the final result long before it took shape beneath his hands.

One summer day I burst into his workroom and found that he was starting to work on some miniature buildings. I knew that he was building regular houses that summer so I never questioned why he was making a miniature village. I just picked up some wood and started to help. I couldn't wait to run to his house each day as our village slowly took shape. We built tiny houses, shops, churches, schools, and fire departments. It was the best fun ever.

Every year, we spent Christmas Eve with Aunt Lena, Uncle Joe, and my cousin Joan. Joan was my idol. The year I was eight, she was twenty-one and I absolutely worshiped her. I loved dressing up in her clothes and playing with her jewelry and makeup. I even went on most all her dates with her! I couldn't wait to grow up so that I could be just like her.

Christmas Eve was almost better than Christmas Day itself. We would walk the short distance to their house, snow crunching underfoot while Dad sang Christmas carols. We would open the door to the front porch and a rush of incredibly delightful smells would overtake us. They used the front porch as an extra refrigerator, so the entry always smelled of lebkuchen and gingersnaps. When we walked in from the cold, it was snuggly warm and friendly.

That Christmas Eve, Uncle Joe met me at the door with a twinkle in his eye. He took my hand and said, "Close your eyes, Jeannie Marie; I have a surprise to show you." I love surprises, so I closed my eyes and let him lead me off. Finally, Uncle Joe told me I could stop and open my eyes.

I gasped in wonder. A winter wonderland lay before me. The parlor off the living room was ablaze with the light of six Christmas trees wrapped in white lights. Spread out around the floor was a complete village with hills and valleys, ice-skating rinks, school buses, and tiny figures shopping and skating. I barely recognized the village that we had so carefully built together. The scene was dotted with millions of little green trees and hundreds of mirrors that sparkled like ice as they reflected the Christmas lights. Oh, it was just magical! He had spent hours attending to every detail to create a fantasy scene for me, and he had done it all with his own hands.

When I think of Uncle Joe, I remember the sense of wonder and magic I felt when I walked into their home that night. He introduced me to the joy of creating something magical out of the simplest of supplies. I still feel the magic. Do your friends feel the magic when they walk into your home?

I often think of him as I sit at my design table surrounded by fabric swatches and appliqués. He taught me to have a vision that I could accomplish anything I wanted. I could have my dream. He used to say that life was like eating a Hershey's Bar. . . . If you eat it all at once, it will come right back up and there will be no joy in it. Eat one square at a time, take time to savor that feeling in your mouth . . . and that Hershey's Bar could last several days. He would say, "Life is to be lived one chunk at a time. Remember, Jeannie Marie, slow and steady wins the race."

We may not all be shining stars . . .
but we can surely twinkle!!!

5

My Baby Brother, Dick

On my fifth birthday, my mom came home from St. Agnes Hospital with a birthday gift for me . . . a brand-new baby brother. Now, I could not understand what everyone was so excited about. I loved, loved, loved being an only child. I just loved everything about it. I think the only one less excited than me about coming home with a new baby was my mom.

Now, keep in mind, my birthday had always been a very important and exciting day in my life. It was always a day I felt like a fairy princess, a day my folks made very special. They would throw a huge birthday party for me and keep it a secret so I was always surprised when I would walk into the backyard and it would be full of all my friends from school and the neighborhood.

I must be a little dense, because I've had many, many surprise parties over the years and I've always fallen for them. The rush that comes when everyone shouts "Surprise!" is better than sex or drugs. Oh, my birthdays have always been magical.

What a black day July 20, 1944, was. My two maiden aunts were taking care of me while my mom was in the hospital. They doted on me for two weeks. I was a happy child until the day before my birthday. They sat me down and explained that mom was coming home on my birthday and would need her rest. That meant peace and quiet and that meant . . . *no big birthday party.*

In the '40s, there were no tantrums, no throwing yourself on the floor ranting and raving, no holding your breath till you turned blue. Oh, no . . . good girls did not do that! Just a single tear ran down my face as my little heart broke. Well, I guess it was more than Aunt Frannie and Aunt Naomi could stand. They jumped in, in a grand style and said, "How about inviting your three best friends to come over for cake and ice cream? We'll just set up a table in the front hall . . . your mom will never hear you there. Just whisper!!!" Oh, well, any excuse for ice cream. I guess it beat nothing. You know, ice cream makes everything better, even big hurts.

I never had another moment in my life where Dick was not attached to my hip. He really was my gift. My mom gave him to me to look after and keep watch over. She was off to work, the only mom I knew who worked in the '40s. And when she wasn't working, she was golfing, bowling, or playing bridge. It was Dick and me against the world. You might think I am making all of this up, but you can ask anyone I hung around with. Why, even at my twenty-fifth class reunion, they all looked around and said, "Hey, Jeanne, where is Dickie?"

I really love my brother very much. We raised ourselves, so we have that closeness. But I treated him miserably. Things I did to him must have been very scary. Like locking him in a closet and shouting that I was packing my suitcase and leaving home and that he would live in the closet by himself forever. Of course, I always released him, gave him a big hug, and sent him on his way. I think I'm blessed he even speaks to me today or that he even talks to any woman. I was sure I had warped him for life.

I can remember when Dickie was a little boy of about two. My mom's best friend, Isla Jikka, came over. She turned to my mom and said, "Mora, I don't know why you ever brought him home from the hospital. He's so tiny, so puny and sickly, and he cries all the time. Why isn't he more like Jeannie Marie? She's so good, so healthy-looking. She's always so happy. She is the perfect child. You should have quit when you were ahead of the game." And I was in total agreement! Oh, why couldn't we just send him back?

Well, no matter what I said or thought, I did pull myself up by my training bra straps and grew to love this little brother more than anything.

And he grew up to be a lesson to me. He's one of the movers and shakers of the world, a real risk-taker. He shows me every day that you can take the leap and grow wings on the way down. He has taken the family business and made it his own, and has taken it to heights my dad never thought possible. He really turned out great, if I do say so myself. He's made me so proud.

One year a dear friend invited my friends and family to celebrate my birthday at Bicé, a great restaurant in Palm Beach. As usual, I was regaling them with the "Fifth Birthday Party" story and how everything was then. When I finished my story, I looked at my brother to say, "Bet you're tired of hearing that story," but before I could get the words out of my mouth, this awful sadness came over me. I think it was the look he had in his eyes, and it dawned on me . . . here sat a man who had never been given a birthday party in his life . . . not one! I don't know why or how it happened, but I realized that moment that it was so. All I could say to him was, "I am so sorry, so sorry." His sadness was a huge lesson to me. Be grateful for what you have, no matter how small . . . it's better than most others will ever get.

On a happier note, last year my sister-in-law, Nancy, threw the two of us the grandest birthday party ever. My mom's five-and-dime kids were now sixty and sixty-five! We had horns, poppers, sparklers, and fireworks. It was my brother's first and my sixty-fifth party. Dick is one of my best friends and for that I am ever grateful.

6

Where Do All the Voices Come From?

I am the biggest chatterbox in the whole world. In fact, I've always said that's how I got a husband. He didn't marry me for my body; he married me for my mouth. He was a very quiet, gentle man and he married me for small talk. I kept his world humming. He always said I needed a listener and that he loved me enough to be that for me.

Now, if you think that I talk a lot, you should be inside my head. My internal chatterbox goes ten times faster. I believe I came equipped with more than the average amount of words and thoughts to use each day. But I do my best to get them all used . . . each day!

Where do our thoughts and beliefs come from? In my world it was a combination of my mom, my dad, and the nuns. I am equal parts saint (from the nuns), bawdy (from my mom), and prude (from my dad). You would think that the two-thirds saint and prude would win out over one-third bawdy, but bawdy is so much more fun! My head is the two-thirds and my mouth is the one-third.

My mom was a free spirit. I always say she could

have been a tramp but she married my dad, "the prude." When my husband was courting me, he would sit at the kitchen table with my mom drinking martinis (it's what people did in the fifties!) and swapping stories. Both of them could tell jokes better than anyone. He thought he was getting a woman like my mom. Alas, after I threw up my first martini, he realized he had married my dad, "the prude."

Yes, all the voices in my head are my dad's sayings. A "Dad's saying" that ruled my life was "Keep your nose to the grindstone; work very hard, struggle, and you'll be a success." Well, for many years, I kept my nose to the grindstone and all I ever got out of the deal was a dirty nose.

Here's a bunch more Dad-isms that still ring between my ears every day:

- "Is the phone ringing? Doing any business? Are you making any money?" Oh, how I hated this ritual. No, I wasn't making any money. But I couldn't tell him I was broke, so I had to become a liar.
- "Jeanne, save your money. Always have enough hidden in the silo to buy a tractor." Now, I never could understand how this applied to me. But my parents went through the depression, the lack during the Second World War, and my mom was born in Scotland. So we were a very frugal family.
- "Jeanne, never count your chickens before they hatch." So I rarely got any joy out of anything be-

cause I was too paranoid to get excited, in case it never came true.

- "Jeanne, know your place in this world; don't get too big for your britches." What he said to me was that middle-class was fine but you don't deserve more. "We are a Ford family." Keep your dreams low-key.

I have a friend who has worked with us over the years and she rates things on a dessert scale. Melted Jell-O with a fly in it is at the low end of the scale. Crème brûlée and Baked Alaska are at the high end. We were taught not to aspire to either end, but to shoot for plain old apple pie—with a hunk of cheese on it if we were feeling lucky. Aim right down the middle. For me to buy into the concept that I could not only have a dream but that I could have a *huge* dream and that I could have it all was a very difficult concept for me to get my arms around. My voices said, "Just settle for a little bit and be grateful."

But inside of me there was this knowing part. A part of me that wanted it all. A part of me that kept reaching for the whole enchilada and then my dad's voice kept pulling me back. A part of me wanted to be loud and bawdy, going for the gusto. But my dad's voice kept saying, "Keep your star hidden under a bushel basket. Be seen, not heard."

This was my struggle for years. Until one day it came to me in a whisper: I am not my dad. I am not my mom. I am not the nuns! It took me sixty years to figure

Where Do All the Voices Come From?

this out. I am ME! I can be the me I want to be. I've taken those voices and have made funny stories of them. I've made good friends of them. Now I fill my head with *my* voice.

Yes, I can have it all. It can be easy. I deserve it all. I am perfect the way I am. My body is what it is. If I can't lose it, I'll decorate it. I'll thank God for my healthy me. *Yeah, me!*

I wish for all of you to find new voices in your head. Make them yours and live them large!

Good Morning!

This is God.
I will be handling all your problems today.
I do not need your help.
So, relax and have a great day!

And . . . really believe!

7

The Cashmere Sweater

Barbara Gores was my dearest bosom buddy as a kid in Wisconsin. We met the first day of kindergarten at Bragg School and we remained friends all the way through high school. We did everything together and were inseparable. We spent hours playing at each other's houses and enjoyed countless giggly sleepovers. You know how when you are best friends with somebody, you trade your things? We had matching little purses, and she would give me hers and I would give her mine. We even shared our first boyfriends. This was the one friend that I shared my whole life with growing up.

To my inexperienced eye, Barbara's family lived in a much higher realm than my family. I knew that they were rich because they ate dinner in the dining room instead of the kitchen. When I ate over we'd sit in the dining room at the table with white cloth napkins on our laps. Her mother would set up the plates in the big galley kitchen and then push through the swinging door between the kitchen and the dining room with the plates in her hands.

I don't remember much about the dinners except that her baked potatoes were always "poofed." I would watch in fascination as Mrs. Gores would cut the potatoes first the long way and then across. She would add butter and salt and pepper. Then she would take her fingers and push it all together and the meat of the potato would go "poof." Somehow even her potatoes were more elegant than regular ones.

As far as I was concerned, Barbara had it all wrapped up in a great big red bow. Barb's dad owned the local Mercury dealership, so when we were sixteen, Barbara got her first of many convertibles. In the four years of high school, Barbara had more cars than I could count. Every day it seemed like there was a new salesman's sample for her to drive. Her first pink convertible gave way to an aqua convertible that was soon replaced with an Edsel. She was the hit of the school. Nobody had an Edsel. My favorite was her red and white Mercury with fluffy dice in the window. On top of it all, her aunt owned a candy factory. What more could you ask for? A friend who had everything and got free candy to boot!

I never envied Barbara any of the things she owned except for her cashmere sweaters. She had fourteen cashmere sweaters in every color of the rainbow. When I first gingerly touched one, I thought that I had never felt anything so luxurious in my life. I wanted a cashmere sweater more than anything in the world. I asked my mom if I could please, please, please have a cashmere sweater. I told her that it would be okay even if it had to be black or white to match our school uniforms. All I wanted was to be able to have a cashmere sweater of my very own. My mom said no. "You know, Jeanne, Barbara has too much. You have to learn that money does not grow on trees. You can't have everything you want." In those days there wasn't the selection in plus sizes that there is today, so my mother made much of my wardrobe. All the pieces were serviceable and there was no room for cashmere.

I didn't get my cashmere sweater, but I think those endless nights of dreaming about piles of beautiful cashmere sweaters motivated me to reach for the stars. I vowed that I would have all the great things the universe had in store for me.

Many years later, when I was married and had enough money to buy my own cashmere sweater, I remember walking into Marshall Field's in downtown Chicago. I walked up to the sweater counter and I reveled in the jewel-like colors. I finally picked out a gorgeous pink one and paid more for it than any other piece of clothing I had ever owned. I was going to be as elegant as Barbara Gores.

Well, wouldn't you know I took it home, wore it once, and broke out with a rash all over my body! What was that commandment about "Thou shalt not covet"? It took me a while, but I finally learned my lesson on that one.

It can be hard when you want something your

friend has. It's hard to rejoice for your friend when she gets something you desperately want. However, when good things happen in our lives, we want our friends to be really happy for us. In truth, there's plenty for every-one. Let's choose to be *that* kind of friend.

Strangers are simply
friends we haven't met

Keep Talking

How do you get to know the people who help along the way on the ol' road to success?

I'm a talker and I come from a whole line of talkers. My dad, Ernie Freund, was the grand champion of talkers. As a child, I was embarrassed by it. He would talk to anyone and everyone, friends and strangers. It didn't matter to him; he just loved to chat with people.

I can remember going to Silver Springs Resort on our family vacation. We were just walking along when all of a sudden my dad shouts out, "Mayville: Mayville, Wisconsin:" He directed it at a man in a wheelchair. Oh, my head whirled with embarrassment. However, the man seemed thrilled to see my dad, and as my dad chatted with him, they laughed and reminisced about old times and all the old business deals they had worked on. They had the best time! And as they finished, the man thanked my dad and said he was happy they had talked. He had been meaning to call him because he had a couple of deals that he wanted to share with my dad. Ol' Ern's offhand chat had just brought in new real estate work that would last him a couple of years.

When my dad started an auction, he never just got up and started selling like most auctioneers did. He would start by talking about the family whose farm he was selling. By the time he was done, you had grown to know and love this family and had felt the worth of their belongings. Then he would talk to the audience, acknowledge old friends and tell a story or two about them. He would seek out the new people and find out why they came. He would always find a couple of people in the crowd who were experts in cows, farm equipment, or antique furnishings. Then, during the sale, he would call on them to back up the value of the piece. "How's it going, Madame Kuony, what do you think this is worth?" It brought a great deal of credibility to the auction and got him a very successful sale time and time again. All by chatting. My dad truly loved people! It was a huge gift that he passed on to me!

I was born with a big mouth and my dad showed me how to use it. I became a chatterbox. Years later when I went into business with my friend Mary Ann, she would warn me over and over to keep my mouth shut. We would get on a plane and by the end of the trip the whole plane knew everyone and their life stories. Mary Ann really hated being in elevators with me. It was close quarters and the people had to talk to me! But years of this chatting has given me knowledge about a lot of little stuff.

I've been kind to lots of people, and they, in turn, have helped me along the way. Don't ever think of it as idle chitchat. Caring about our fellow man is worth millions. Keep talking!

Why Did the Duck Fly Upside Down?

Because He Was Always Quacking Up!!

9

Life's Gravy

This is one of those lessons that has showed me that all there is left to do sometimes is to pull myself up by my bra straps and get on with it.

I got married between my third and fourth year of college. My husband was beginning his fifth year. From the date of our wedding in June until September when school started, we needed a place to live. My brother-in-law Ralph and his wife, Ev, were moving to their house on the Fox River for the summer. They very sweetly offered us their house in town until we moved on to school. For our rent, I would have to cook Ralph lunch Monday through Friday, and Ev suggested I make it a hearty one so she didn't have to feed him again at night. Now, keep in mind, I had been cooking for my family since I was twelve years old, and I, along with my dear, sweet dad, believed I was the bestest cook in the whole wide world.

On our honeymoon, however, I'd had a devastating experience. In 1959, honeymoons were very important. You finally got to have sex, so Butchie felt two weeks in the north woods of Wisconsin with nothing to do but stay in bed and play the whole time would be perfect. Little did I know that two weeks of anything in the north woods is way too long for anything, even sex. After all,

1. I was a virgin
2. There were bears in the backyard
3. It rained the whole time . . . poured!
4. It was freezing cold
5. I got pleurisy and landed flat on my back (at first it was diagnosed as too much sex, which I was in agreement with, but then they found an infection)
6. The one decent restaurant in the area served only frog legs, and after six days of frog legs, my new husband literally turned green!

So, I finally had to cook. Now, what does one cook on a cold, rainy day in Wisconsin? Chili! Oh, perfect! My dad loved my chili. I made a huge batch. We needed good comfort food to get us through the next week since the pleurisy took away the reason for being here . . . sex, sex, sex!!!!

I set the table and put a bowl of pinecones and greens in the center . . . oh, I felt like the perfect housewife. Wisconsin chili is more like a soup and we dunk buttered rye bread in the juice. So, I shopped for the perfect bread, made a beautiful stack of buttered slices, and filled a great, big bowl with chili for us to share . . . we were honeymooners, you know! Well, my new husband took a big taste and spit it right across the room, screaming, "What the hell is this?" Through tears I explained that it was chili. Well, it was not like his mom's chili. So with that the honeymoon was over . . . I wanted to go home! I wanted my mom and dad. I wanted my old life back.

At this point in my life I became a little sensitive about my cooking.

So, when I was given the task of cooking a lunch a day for my brother-in-law Ralph, I stepped up to the

challenge. The first noon I served baked chicken with mashed potatoes and green beans (out of the can). Again, I was so proud of my huge lunch. The table was outstanding. I was sure he had never had such a beautiful meal.

Well, when we sat down and helped ourselves, we did not have enough gravy. I only had enough pan juices to make about half a cup of gravy. Ralph did not notice my chicken was roasted to golden brown and my potatoes were lumpless, but laughed and laughed about the lack of gravy. I licked my wounds and vowed to do better the next day. I created the most gorgeous pot roast with oven-browned potatoes, carrots, and sweet, juicy onions. And today, I had gotten a perfect cup of gravy! Again the perfection was overlooked. All that was noticed was that we still didn't have enough gravy!

That day I pulled myself up by my bra straps and decided I would master gravy. At the end of the summer, I could make gravy for five hundred out of nothing, and I do not use bouillon cubes. (Someday I will do a cookbook and share my secret with you.)

Now, I am one of the greatest cooks in the world. If you believe in yourself, you too can become a master of gravy and anything else in life you choose.

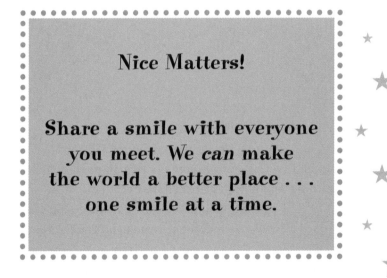

Nice Matters!

Share a smile with everyone
you meet. We *can* make
the world a better place . . .
one smile at a time.

10

I'm Jeanne Bice

When Butch and I married in 1959, it seemed like the perfect time to be alive; a glorious time to be newly-weds. My friends and I felt like the sky was the limit in terms of how we would be able to improve on the world that our parents had created. Confidence was in the air—we just knew that we would succeed.

We set up housekeeping in Ripon, Wisconsin, my husband's hometown. Ripon was a small town of about five thousand people who all appeared to me to already know and care about one another. All the friendships seemed to have been formed years ago, leaving me as the odd man out. I was new to marriage and to mother-hood and was so very young. I missed my friends to guide me in the ways of my new life.

One day, shortly after we had settled in, my father-in-law asked me to take a walk with him down to the lake. My father-in-law was a very successful business-man and was well known locally as a stern man who ruled his home with an iron hand. I had discovered a tendency within myself to blurt out exactly the wrong thing at the worst possible time when I was around him, so I worked hard to stay out of his way. There have been few people in life able to intimidate me but he was certainly one of them. I was terrified but this offer of a walk was not negotiable. So I summoned my courage, pulled myself up yet again by my bra straps, and agreed to meet him for a "chat."

> Triumph is just a little *umph* added to *try*.

I had steeled myself against his inevitable advice-giving, so when he stopped and turned to me, his words startled me. "Jeanne, what are your plans?" My mind went blank as I cast around for a suitable answer. I had no plans. I was married and that was enough. Sensing my confusion, he continued that I was now responsible for the social portion of our lives as a married couple. It would be my role to build friendships and create a social circle.

The thought of having to make friends petrified me, since I had never consciously had to seek out friends. As a child, my friends evolved naturally from relationships in school and among the kids in the neighborhood. Even when I left for college, roommates were assigned to me, so I made friends out of them. I had no idea how to tackle this monumental task.

My father-in-law must have seen the stricken look on my face and taken pity. His next words have served me well over the past several decades. "Smile at everyone you meet. Say hello and act as if they're already your friends. They will assume that they know you, and very soon the whole town will love you."

I've been following this same advice for the past forty years and it has carried me through hundreds of new experiences. My father-in-law died shortly after my first wedding anniversary. I regret that I was too young and intimidated to get to know him better and to become his friend.

What a waste of time fear is! As you go through your life today, remember that everyone has something to teach.

Hi, I'm Jeanne Bice. I'm glad to meet you.

Believe in Yourself

and

Magic Will Happen!!!

11

One Friend Leads to Another

My mom was a girlfriend expert. She had many, and for all occasions. I learned the importance of friendship through her example. She had her bowling girlfriends, her bridge girlfriends, her gardening girlfriends, her lunch girlfriends, and her traveling girlfriends.

She always used to say, "Don't forget your girlfriends. They become more important to you as the years go on. No matter how much you love your husband and family, you are still going to need girlfriends. Go places with them, do things with them. You'll need other women . . . women always do!"

I followed her advice, and gathered my girlfriends. I got more and more each year. As the years went on, I gradually came to understand that my mom really knew what she was talking about. Girlfriends have become a huge part of my life. After sixty-some years of living in this world, here is what I know about girlfriends.

Girlfriends listen when your heart is breaking. Girlfriends will give you a party on every occasion of your life. They are there for you when the men in your life let you down. They cry with you when someone dies. Girl-friends are there during the hard times, and the good times. They are happy with you when you are happy, and are sad when you are sad. Girlfriends will drive through blizzards, rainstorms, and the gloom of night to help you clean out your mom's cupboards after she dies. And they're the ones who make you keep a few pieces for memory's sake, even if you just want to pitch it all.

Time passes, life happens, and children grow up and leave home. Marriages fail, loves come and go, and hearts break. Careers end, parents die, and men don't call. But girlfriends are there, no matter where they live or what is going on in their lives. The world would not be as much fun without them, and neither would I!

I've made several different sets of girlfriends over the years. I always thought it would be great if they could all be one big happy group, but as I matured I re-alized life just doesn't work that way and now I relish them for their differences.

Come meet some of the girlfriends I made as a young mother in Ripon, Wisconsin, back in the '70s. They are still special friends in my life and they show me all the time that Mom was right. We need girl-friends.

When I was a young mother I had a group of friends, most of whom were older than me. The joy of being with them was that they had walked the road of life I hadn't yet traveled. They knew all about the trials and tribulations of raising children and they were living proof that you do survive! They taught me that you can have it all in life, just maybe not all at once. Give it some time and patience . . . the world is your apple, eat it one bite at a time. Long before I hit menopause, they showed me my future with hot flashes, and taught me that only humor can get you through it! They would get up in the middle of a bridge game, stand at the front door in the dead of winter, and fan themselves. Steam would rise. We all shared the discomfort, but it did bring on gales of laughter.

One of the women in this group was the most gorgeous, sophisticated woman you've ever seen. She wore her hair pulled back very tight into a huge bun in the back of her head. She was elegant. Every so often you would see little beads of perspiration sneak up from her scalp. She taught us to keep our dignity, no matter how bad it gets!

I love this group so much. Ruth, June, Gladys, Henrietta, Joyce, Hildy, Ellie, and Marilyn. Since then some have died, and like me, some have moved away, but we are girlfriends forever. Every time I have a flash, I send them my love.

Then there was my age group. Donna, Joan, Jenny, Claire, Beth, and Nancy. There were many more and you know who you are. These are the friends I raised my children with. They were the glue of my life and show up time and again throughout these stories. I love them beyond words and I am who I am in large part because of them.

And then there was a group of the young ones. There were five of us: Patty, Mary Ann, Sherri, Jane, and me. We were all married with children. We played as girlfriends and did stuff as couples. All of us truly believed we were living the American Dream. We had it all, and it was wrapped up in a pink polka-dot bow. We had homes of our own, husbands with great jobs, and the perfect kids. We were stay-at-home moms. We shopped, we did charity work, we coffeed, we were in love with our lives—everything was perfect! Or, was it??

Within a few short years we were all single. We either divorced or were widowed. We were on our own trying to pull it all back together again.

In 1981 Mary Ann and I moved to Florida. We had opened a new Silent Woman shop in Boca Raton, FL. On our first winter there we decided we all needed a little R&R, so we invited Patty, Sherry, and Jane down to Boca for a little fun in the sun. It would be a cheap vacation—Mary Ann and I lived next door to each other in a condo on the beach. "Y'all come down and we'll share our joys and tears."

Over twenty years we have continued to share a week or so together each year. Many changes have occurred in our lives. Boyfriends have come and gone, new husbands have been invited into our lives. Kids have married and many wonderful grandchildren have followed. Through all the joys and sadness of these years, we have remained true friends. We've been there with free advice, sure, but most of all we've just been there with gobs of love for one another. We are the one constant in each of our lives.

Without each of these groups of girlfriends I am certain I would not have survived. I love each and every one of them and I thank them for being my friends.

"Sometimes listening is just as . . . . . . important as talking. Call anytime!"

I believe a friend is God's way of proving He doesn't want us to walk through life alone.

12

Movin' On Up

When our kids were still small, several of us girls would get together for coffee every morning. It wasn't long before our conversation turned to our desire to better ourselves, to become more active socially. We all agreed that the one thing local high society was missing was us! We needed a way to move up in our town's social ranks.

We *needed* to play *bridge*.

After a little detective work, we discovered Cora and Cappy Jasper were the best players in town and we decided they would teach us.

As a group we marched over and knocked on their door. Cora invited us in and quickly got us perched on her sofa, drinking tea. Soon all of us were talking and interrupting one another as we shared our strategy. In the middle of our commotion Cora began chuckling and by the end she was laughing out loud at our enthusiasm. We told her that we would like to have a bridge club. We told her about all the things that we would like to have along with it. But most of all, we told her, we wanted to be women who played bridge.

Thankfully, Cora agreed, and every week eight of us faithfully showed up at her house. Slowly but surely we were learning how to play. Thursday nights soon became the highlight of our week. After each lesson, we would get home flushed with laughter and anxious to practice our bidding. We were having a blast! In the mornings after our bridge lesson, we'd sit down at someone's kitchen table. There were always at least four of us and we would practice with our kids running in and out, crawling under our feet at the table. The house might be in an uproar, but we were happy becoming "women who played bridge."

After Cora declared our lessons complete, we officially started our bridge club. It was even better than we had originally imagined. Bridge gave us a whole new outlook on life. It got us away from the daily drudgery of the diapers in the washing machine, the endless rounds of housecleaning, and the strain of having to be smart enough to help the kids with their homework. It was the original Girls' Night Out.

I think these bridge parties were a large part of our growing up. You know, in the '60s and '70s, sometimes it was hard to feel like a grown-up. These parties gave us confidence. Our social lives centered around bridge. It was always an evening full of fun, laughter, and chatter. If you're looking for a treat for yourself—something that you, you and your husband, or you and your best girlfriends can do—find a bridge game and join in. It may seem just like a hand of cards, but I have the most wonderful memories of playing with my dearest girlfriends.

13

An Old-Fashioned Christmas

"Everybody loves somebody . . ."

This was a line from a song in my teen years: and I loved everybody! Back then I did love everybody, and I just knew everybody loved me. I was outgoing, kind, a real do-gooder. I had a heart full of enough love for the whole world, and I gave it freely. So, when I found out the whole world did not love Jeanne Bice, it was a very black day in my life.

When I lived in Wisconsin I was very involved with the Ripon Women's Club. One of the projects that I took on was a tour of homes. I did the first tour. Ripon, Wisconsin, is the birthplace of the Republican Party, and a historic little town with lots of old, historic homes. It is a beautiful place to have a tour of homes, and I was excited to run it that year. It was a huge success. We had bus tours between the homes and I would ride the bus and give little talks to the people. I'd share with them the whole history of the town while taking them from stop to stop and then they had the joy of touring the wonderful, grand old home.

So, the next year, the woman who became chairman of the tour asked me to open my home to the public. The theme that year was "An Old-Fashioned Christmas," and our home was noted for our Christmas decorations. At Christmastime, people came from all over to look at our main Christmas tree. We lived on a corner, so they could see it from the front of the house and the side view from our living room. We had a room with sixteen-foot ceilings and the tree filled this room. It had thousands and thousands of tiny white lights and hundreds and hundreds of glass ornaments. It took Butch a full week to decorate it. One summer I had some electrical work done. When I asked the electrician how much I owed him, he responded that he just wanted to be invited into our home sometime after dark during Christmas so he could see the tree close-up. He said that he would call it a fair deal and "even-steven" if we did. He did get his invite, and our families became great friends.

I thought and thought about opening my house to the tour of homes. I realized that it wasn't fair of me to ask all those other people who made my tour of homes such a success to open their homes if I wasn't willing to do it myself. So, as a family we agreed to do it. We had so much fun . . . we decorated the house and it was gorgeous. We were all ready, and the day of the tour of homes was a huge success. Gobs of people went through our home. I knew the house was going to be all decorated, so I planned to have a group of people in for a party after the tour was over. The committee came in, and we got everything all cleaned up. Not a thing was harmed, and not a piece of anything was out of place when they left. The house was ready for Christmas in all of its glory.

In walked all my friends and we sat around and re-hashed the day. We had dinner and it was just a joyful time. About halfway through the evening, the doorbell by the breezeway rang. I got up and walked to the breezeway door, but there was no one there. I opened the door and looked around and still saw no one, but there was a note on the door. Since there was no one

there, I started reading the note, figuring that someone must have just had something to say. It was the worst note I had ever read in my life. In essence it said, "I don't like you . . . who in the hell do you think you are that you can open your home up and show it to everyone in town and brag, brag, puff your cheeks, brag, brag, puff your cheeks . . ." Again, the fear of my father's voice rang in my head. "Don't ever puff your cheeks, because if you puff your cheeks you will fail." I thought, "I bragged about my house, I put it on the tour of homes! I puffed my cheeks, and now the whole world hates me!"

I sat down at the kitchen table, and my husband said, "It's just a note, Jeanne."

"There's somebody in this world who doesn't love me!" I said.

"I'm sure there are *lots* of people in this world who don't love you. You yourself admit that you have a big mouth and are constantly butting into people's lives. Not everybody likes that. Get over yourself." I sat there and thought, "My God, not everybody loves me . . . how can that be? I'm a good person, I do wonderful things for people, and I'd give up my own life for someone else. How could they possibly not love me?"

Butch sat down and gently put his arm around me. He told me not to worry about the ones who didn't love me. He told me to revel in the joy of the ones who *do*.

"Look at the friends that you have in your life. Look at all the people you touch and who touch you every day, and how much joy you bring to each other. You

There's always going to be the fish
that gets away.

GONE FISHIN'

can't worry about the fish that got away. There is always going to be the fish that gets away. What you have to do is sit down and enjoy the fish dinner that you did catch that day."

That was a real lesson for me. It took me a long time to get over the fact that I couldn't please everybody. I spent my whole life trying to do that, but I think that for those of us who learn this lesson, life is a lot easier. Not everyone wants to be your friend, but take the ones that you have, wrap your arms around them, and thank them!

Fake It Till You Believe It...
Fake It Till You Make It

Most of us live with a trace of unworthiness! We live our days criticizing ourselves even more than others. Why pick on yourself? We are our own worst enemies sometimes.

I deserve it

I deserve it

I deserve it

I deserve it

I am worthy

I am worthy

I am worthy

I am worthy

Say it over and over and over and the funny thing is, you really begin to believe it. I know it's a funny concept, but we need to treat ourselves better than we treat everyone else.

This was a hard thing for me to grasp. I was raised by nuns and was taught to treat everyone wonderfully. So, the butcher, the baker, and the Indian chief get good strokes from me. I praise everyone. I tell them what a good job they've done, raise their spirits all the time. I help give them wings to fly. No one ever said, "Do the same for yourself." Why, that sounded selfish to me. I couldn't do that.

This is just "Stinking Thinking." And you want to know what really stinks: I not only don't praise myself, I kick myself when I'm down and jump up and down on the remains of my spirit. For years I clipped my own wings so I could not fly. No flying for Jeanne, she's stupid, fat, a flibbertygibbet. Someone needs to take care of me.

So now I, too, say:

I deserve it
I deserve it
I deserve it
And now I believe it!

14

Angels Don't Always Wear Wings

One day, I got a knock at my door. It was Patty, a gal that I knew from Women's Club. She had taken the position of vice-president in charge of projects. Her job was to bring new and innovative projects to the club to earn money. They were going to do a charity ball that year and she said I was the first person she thought of to run it. Would I do it?

I politely declined. With two kids and a job, it seemed to me like it would be a huge project. She suggested that I co-chair with another woman from the club, Mary Ann. I said no way! Apparently, Patty had gone to Mary Ann with the same proposal and Mary Ann had said much the same thing, and she told Patty she couldn't work with me because I was a snob. I thought Mary Ann was a bitch. Patty thought the combination could be great and, after much begging, groveling, and promising to cook for us for a week (she was a very good cook), asked if we would give it a try as a favor to her. Reluctantly we both agreed.

Sometimes first judgments and opinions have to be

eaten later in life! I will say that I did come to eat my words. It took only one meeting for Mary Ann and I to become the very best of friends. We admired each other's strengths and discovered that we had more in common than we had ever imagined.

The charity ball was a huge success and it birthed a friendship that has lasted my whole life. Mary Ann and I became family. After the ball, we branched out. First we started shopping together and then started taking craft classes. It became almost a competition to see who could do something better and faster. We traveled to Milwaukee, Fond du Lac, and Oshkosh until we became two of the best crafters in the area. Cooking classes were next, and they kept our interest for several years. Finally we realized that you can only craft, cook, and shop so much!

One day Mary Ann said, "Jeanne, I'm ready. Let's go into business." I didn't know what to say, so I told her that I would check my horoscope the next day and see what advice it gave. The next morning my horoscope said something like, "You are on the edge of a great, new project. It will be enormously successful for you." Honest to God, that is the truth. I called Mary Ann and I told her that we were going into business together. We did, however, forget to go to business school. We were just two relatively pampered housewives. Luckily we had husbands anxious to bankroll us if it kept us busy and out of their hair.

We were in business for about a year and a half

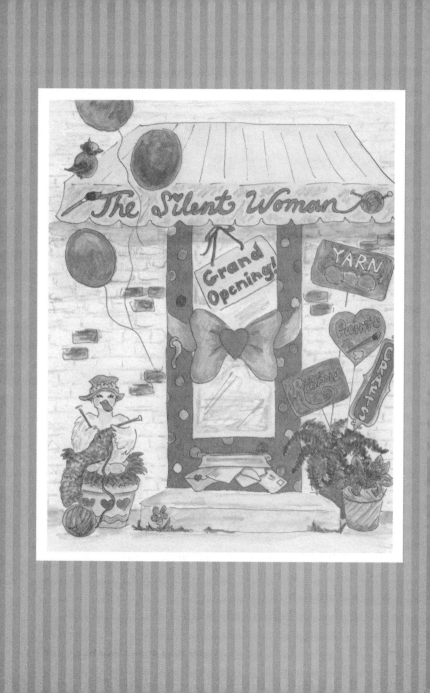

when Mary Ann decided that her marriage was over. What had been a hobby suddenly had to be able to support her and the children. Within a year, my husband died and *both* of us had to make a living out of the business.

God certainly works in strange ways. I never wanted to be in business. Mary Ann and I went into business on an absolute lark and the result became the mainstay and support of our lives. Our shop was truly a gift from God. Mary Ann and I helped raise each other's kids and helped each other figure out where we were going and how to get there.

Sometimes when you think something isn't going to work out or isn't going to be the way it should be, you should step back. God has plans for us that are greater than we could ever dream or expect. He often performs miracles in very strange and quacky ways.

There is an old joke where the man is in a flood and he climbs out onto the roof of his porch and a rowboat comes by. The guy in the rowboat asks the man if he can give him a ride. But the man just tells him that he is waiting for God to save him. The water gets higher and higher. Soon a big powerboat comes by and the owner offers the man a lift. Again, the man tells him that he is waiting for God to save him. Pretty soon he is up on the top of the chimney with the water almost covering him. A helicopter comes by and asks the man if he wants a lift. The man says that he is waiting for God to save him

When you think something isn't going to work . . .

. . . you should step back, because God has plans for us that are greater than we could ever dream.

with a miracle. The water finally reaches him and the man drowns.

When the man gets to heaven, he meets God and asks Him, "Well, what happened? You always said you would save me!" God said, "I sent you a rowboat, a powerboat, and a helicopter! What were you waiting for?"

Sometimes we just forget that miracles are waiting to happen every single moment of our lives. All we have to do is open our hearts and minds to reach up and grab them. Sometimes the message is sent to us over and over. If we are closed off, God's special plan for us can just float by. Open up your heart and mind to the miracles all around us, and you will experience the provision of a loving God.

Mary Ann was one of the many miracles God sent to me. Without her and our business, I don't know where I would be today. I am so grateful to Patty for bringing me and Mary Ann together. Angels don't always come with wings. Sometimes they show up with the name Patty, wearing funky clothes and sporting perky haircuts!

Angels carry us around
by our bra straps.

15

Coffee Break

Every day I still have fear. I don't have "great big gobs of panic," but I always have fears. Whenever they come up, I ask God to take them for me. Fear freezes forward motion. There are so many truly wonderful things to experience in life; it is a shame to pass them by because of fear.

Back in the late '50s and early '60s when I started my family, the times were much simpler. There were few two-income households, no computers, and not even a word for terrorists. Our lives today are more complex, stressful, and downright scarier. And we are all so busy, we seem to have forgotten about some of our most basic needs as human beings.

When I was a young housewife and mother, a group of us used to get together two or three mornings a week for a cup of coffee. It was a good two- to three-hour break where we threw the kids together to do their thing, and we sat in the kitchen and talked. We weren't just squeezing it in. It was what we were there to do. A time to sit, relax, and share. Think of the last time you

did that. This was a place where you could go when you were all wrapped up in the trials of living in your world. A place where you could hear about what a shit *her* husband was or how bad *that* kid was being. A place where, pretty soon, you were laughing and feeling better about how good you really had it. It was a time for counting our blessings. It was a ceremony. We respected it, we reveled in it, and we looked forward to it. How sad that today we would look at this kind of leisurely get-together as a luxury, an extra, or something to squeeze in when we can.

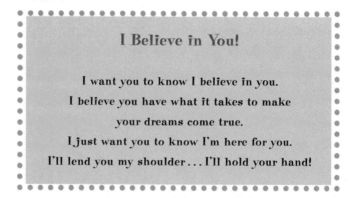

I Believe in You!

I want you to know I believe in you.
I believe you have what it takes to make
your dreams come true.
I just want you to know I'm here for you.
I'll lend you my shoulder . . . I'll hold your hand!

I can't see that, in the last thirty years, our humanness has changed. Just the demands that life puts on us. So here we go, girls, come onna my house and I'll bake a cake. Let's have fun, coffee, and girl talk. Don't just do it for you, don't just do it for me, do it for us. So we can all have a more joyous experience of this great gift that is life.

16

Be Careful What You Wish For

When I was eight years old, I wanted a red bicycle and a new pair of roller skates more than life itself. My mother was not a believer in children having a lot of stuff, and always met my pleas with the same excuses: "You'll fall and knock your teeth out." "Jeanne, you're a klutz, you'll kill yourself!" Or the perennial "Maybe when you're older." My entire childhood seemed to be comprised of one long "Wait until you're older."

Spring was always the toughest time, since the first sunny day signaled to all the neighborhood children that it was finally time for them to break out their Christmas bikes and skates. Finagling my friends into letting me ride their bikes for a few minutes became almost a full-time job. I've come to believe that God was using these negotiations not only to exercise my gift for gab but also increase my imagination since I had very little to bargain with at the time.

Every so often my efforts would be successful. As soon as I was astride the borrowed bike, I would race down the sidewalk like the wind! My heart would swell

with pride at my prowess. I was good! How I wished my mother could see what a great bike rider I was! If I had my own bike, I just knew that I could be a world-class biker.

The only obstacles were my mother . . . and the neighborhood trenches.

Reach for the moon . . .
the least that can happen is you fall among the stars.

Our across-the-street neighbors were an ancient brother and sister who took a lot of pride in their yard. The brother edged that lawn within an inch of its life, creating deep furrows that bordered the entire yard and trenches that ran down both sides of the sidewalk. These trenches seemed to have a magnetic attraction for any bike I happened to be riding. No sooner would I ride past the old people's yard than the bike and I would inexplicably tumble into the nearest trench.

Usually I could call and call my mother and never get an answer. But somehow the atmospheric shift of my crash would alert her, and within seconds she would be out the door yelling, "Did you knock your teeth out? They're the only ones you'll get!" I would look at the tangle of bike and leg and just know that I wouldn't be getting a bike of my own until my friends were getting cars.

Many years later, I told my friend Mary Ann this story and she said, "Let's go buy ourselves a couple of bikes! It'll be fun and we can ride together." I knew instantly the bike I wanted. It had to be a bright-red, ten-speed Schwinn with a basket on the front. My heart almost beat out of my chest the day my husband picked it up and brought it home. It was still such a big deal for me even at the ripe old age of forty! I couldn't contain my excitement as Butch methodically assembled it—I think I even had a hot flash in celebration.

That very night, Mary Ann and I had our maiden voyage. We chose a route that was not too hilly and wound through the neighborhood waving to our startled friends and ringing our bike bells in joy. After our ride, I very carefully dusted my bike off and covered it with a blanket before putting it in the garage. It was my very own bike and even though I didn't ride as fast as an eight-year-old did, I loved it. Every day I would go to work knowing that at 6:30 that night Mary Ann would be in my driveway, ringing her bell and saying, "Come on, Bice, get a move on. Let's ride!"

After a week we decided to expand our horizons and ride through downtown. We rode up Woodside Avenue and then took a right to head over to Main Street. As we stopped in front of Ripon Drug, we chatted with several people about our great new bikes. As I pressed on the right pedal to start off again, the pedal suddenly sheered off, catapulting me backward over the fender. My head hit the street with a mighty thud so hard my teeth rattled. As everyone fluttered around me trying to pick me up, I swear I heard my mother's voice saying, "Told you so!"

Bikes are like horses. If you fall off, you have to get right back up if only to obscure the fact that you just made a huge fool of yourself. We refused many kind offers of a ride. Mary Ann and I pushed our bikes all the way home that night, laughing hysterically at the look of shock on my face when I hit the ground. Butch didn't fix the bike pedal before the first snow flew, which was just as well since it took weeks for my joints to heal and my fanny to recover.

That Christmas we spent in Florida and I suffered the worst toothache of my life. We awoke my mother's dentist out of bed and I had to have three emergency root canals. The dentist couldn't understand how my teeth had been so damaged and asked if I had recently been in a car accident or fallen off a ladder—anything that might have weakened my teeth. My mother looked me in the eye and said, "That damned bike!"

Over the next few years I had fifteen root canals and all my back teeth capped as a result of my mishap. Butch wanted to submit my story to *Ripley's Believe It or Not!* as support for his claim that I was the owner of the most expensive bike in the world.

Sometimes there's a cost to living your dreams. For me, fulfilling the dream of my childhood had its price in modern dentistry. I would pay that price several times over for the joy of those days. Even now, I have the most wonderful memories of the wind blowing in my hair. Nothing can dim the sweet joy of riding my very own bike down the street with Mary Ann, waving and smiling. Mostly I remember our giggly walk home that night. Mary Ann stuck by me although I had made a fool of both of us. She could have gotten home much more quickly by riding her bike, but she laughed and pushed her bike alongside me as I hobbled. True friends encourage your dreams and help you to make them a reality. True friends walk with you through good times and bad. Mary Ann is one of those true friends.

WORLD CLASS

1st

Jeanne Freund

17

The Asparagus Caper

It's spring . . . time to hit the highways and byways. And, of course, it's time for my best friends, Mrs. Bischoff and Mrs. Long, to coerce me into going asparagus hunting with them. You may be familiar with lobster season in South Florida or truffle hunts in Provence, France, but until you have engaged in a spirited search for fresh asparagus, I would hesitate to consider you a real food connoisseur.

That said, I am one of the few people in the world who doesn't like fresh asparagus. I love it right from the can . . . hot or cold . . . white or green . . . whether standing at the counter eating it with my fingers or at a very formal dinner party. But spring is spring, and when your best friends say it's time to go out and walk the back roads and old railroad tracks to find brand-new, fresh asparagus . . . mmmm. God forbid I should be left out of anything, so I always go along. But I drive the car for a speedy escape, just in case! My love for canned asparagus requires only a quick trip to the local market for me to satisfy it. A yearning for fresh asparagus requires a spirit of adventure, a fast car, and some partners in crime.

Wild asparagus is to be found growing on the back roads of Wisconsin. For some reason, the most sought-after clumps are often found around old railroad ties on someone else's property. Once you've discovered the best areas, their locations are guarded fanatically. Even the fact that a farmer wielding a shotgun ran you off last year from the same spot doesn't dissuade you from venturing back this year to reap your spoils.

A good friend will come and bail you out of jail . . . but a true friend will be sitting next to you saying, "Damn . . . that was fun!"

You must always cut the stalks. Pulling the stalks out ruins the roots for next year's crop and will cause you to be banished from the fellowship of asparagus hunters. (Then again, a bunch of wild-eyed women packing sharp knives may not be the best company to keep.)

If all this talk of asparagus has awakened a burning desire within you to hunt and gather asparagus for yourself, I offer you the following suggestions as an expert.

#1. You need a sense of adventure. You are often hunting on property whose ownership is debatable. Is it public domain or does the farmer who happens to live there own it? Is it your asparagus or his? The International Council of Asparagus Hunters handbook states clearly that if it's outside his fence, it's ours for the picking. But you must have a fast car in case the farmer that lives there hasn't referred to his International Council of Asparagus Hunters handbook recently!

#2. You must be fearless. Fearless of snakes and all the creepy crawly things that live in the ditches next to the farmer's fence. No one is ever allowed to scream, no matter what they see. It causes fear, which leads to giggling, which inevitably tests our final rule.

#3. ALWAYS REMEMBER to go to the bathroom before you leave the house.

What is the yield of a trip like this? Lots of wonderful memories with your best friends that you can laugh about for years, and about a half a cup of the spring vegetable. But they say it is the food of the gods . . . not to be shared with anyone but your very best friends. I believe them.

Speaking of best friends, is it possible to find blessings as exciting and unique as those that happen with our closest friends in the simplest of circumstances? Open up for and believe in blessings and they will happily appear. It is the way God made them.

Cream of Asparagus Soup

1 pound of asparagus
2 tablespoons butter
2 tablespoons flour
3 pints white stock
1 pint milk
salt, pepper, ground nutmeg
pinch sugar
1/4 pint cream
4 ounces of cream cheese
handful of mixed cooked green peas and diced beans

DIRECTIONS:

Clean the asparagus and cut off the tips. Cook the tips carefully until soft and put aside for use as a garnish. Cut the stalks into small pieces and wash thoroughly in cold, salted water. Boil in salted water until just tender. Drain. Heat the butter and slowly add the flour. Gradually add the stock and milk, stirring continuously. Bring to a boil, skim if necessary, and add the asparagus stalks, salt, pepper, and nutmeg and pinch of sugar. Cook gently until stalks are very soft. Rub mixture through a sieve or puree in a blender. Add more milk if required, and bring liquid to a boil. Stir the cream and cream cheese into the soup. Add peas, beans, and asparagus tips and serve.

May be served hot or cold.

If cold, remember to add the cream after the soup is chilled.

18

Snowstorm

There is nothing like a huge blizzard in the state of Wisconsin. You can feel it in the air before you even get out of bed. Kids all wait expectantly for those magic words: "There's a big one coming, kids. Put on your boots and go build a snowman! No school today!" We would all wander down to the living room in our pajamas and slippers to watch the blizzard race across the park toward our house. The snow would rise higher and higher until everything was just lumps under a white blanket. I have pictures of my kids, Terry Lee and Tim, with their fingers only inches from the power lines that ran by our house. I deny ever telling them that the lines were for swinging!

Blizzard days were always quiet, beautiful days. Only a very few things could persuade us to leave the comfort of our fire to venture out into the cold. If I was out of milk or bread, Butch would don his wool coat with the fur-lined hood and trek to the grocery for our emergency provisions. Butch was 6'4", so he was quite a sight against the blinding white of the landscape. I think

he looked forward to the chance to show the kids and me his Nanook of the North Woods look.

Another thing that would rouse us from our warm cocoon was a call from the employees at the radio station we owned. We had a mammoth snowmobile and we were often pressed into service to ferry employees back and forth from home to the station before the snowplows were able to clear the roads. I think most of the employees hoped it would be Butch who was sent to retrieve them since I was notorious for my ability to carve new roads where none had existed before. Blizzard days were days for laughter and fun and helping others to make it through.

As the blizzard would begin to subside, the sun would come out and the world would become so still. The sunlight would glisten off the ice on the trees and everything would be absolutely gorgeous.

I would wait for the phone to ring and invariably it would be our neighbor Hildy Rupenow. She would say, "We've got a fire going, Jeanne. Why don't you come on over, have supper and a couple of hands of bridge?"

I'd open up the freezer and pull out some dessert or a casserole. I'd throw a jar of pickles and a jar of fruit preserves into a basket and we would set out for the Rupenows' house. In those days, you always had the equivalent of a whole cow and lots of chickens in your freezer. In the summer, you would spend days canning or "putting up" every possible fruit and vegetable. Now was the chance to enjoy the benefits of all that work. Between the freezer and the larder, I had enough food to feed an entire third-world country.

Our street was always one of the last to be plowed. The kids would already be outside building snowmen and making snow angels, bundled up so that only their eyes were showing. Often the only way you could tell which ones were yours was by their relative size. They would be having the time of their lives running and laughing, falling down and laughing some more.

Butch and I would wave as we trekked across the street. We were off to share some laughter with our own friends. Since we couldn't go to work, we might as well take our cue from the children and declare it a "friend" day.

We'd knock on the Rupenows' door and they would open up with faces shiny from the heat of the fire. "Doncha just love blizzards?" We'd laugh and walk into their warm house. The fireplace would be roaring and we were soon nicely toasted. They had a big picture window that looked right across the street, so we could watch the kids building their snowmen. It was perfect— we could share the children's joy while sharing some time with good friends.

Friends are like links in a chain. Each has its own strength and beauty. I felt that Hildy and Babe Rupenow were special friends and I knew that we would share many blizzard days for years to come. But I never imagined the unique role that God would have Hildy play in my life until I got a call in the middle of the night. It was Hildy screaming, "Jeanne, come quick! Hurry! Babe died, Babe died." On that day, Hildy Rupenow taught me a lesson I would too quickly need to use myself—how to be a widow.

I threw on a coat and my boots while I yelled to Butch that Hildy needed me. Hildy had no family or relatives in town, but she was surrounded by good friends. I was so young and I had never been around anyone who had lost a loved one. I didn't know what to say or what to do to help to ease her pain. I stayed with her for four seemingly endless days as I watched her bury someone she loved. I learned what it was like to sit and listen to friends who came to give you love in the form of endless casseroles. I watched as the town surrounded Hildy with its love and propped her up during those days of grief. Sometimes we would talk about the joy of life with Babe, but often we would just sit in silence. Never did I imagine that a few years later I would be forced to rely on the lessons I learned that week.

Hildy didn't live very long after Babe died. I'm convinced that she died of a broken heart. I think this happens in a lot of families when you have two people whose lives are so tightly intertwined. It is such a time of pain when you lose the love of your life. Grief can be a terrifying and hideous companion. I've learned through my own painful experiences that unless you really put yourself in God's hands, the grief can get the best of you. Hildy taught me how to handle the death of a loved one, but she also taught me to heal my broken heart so that I could live. If I hadn't, it would have killed me, too.

Remember, when friends gather, it warms your heart and soul. Enjoy every moment of them because you don't know how long you are going to have them. Welcome the unexpected interruptions in your schedule. When a friend calls and says, "I've got a roaring fire going," take time to sit with them and enjoy the moment. You'll be making memories for a lifetime.

19

Life Sometimes Takes You to Pickett, Wisconsin

The point of life's journey is not to arrive at the grave safely with a well-preserved body, but rather to skid in sideways, totally worn-out, shouting, "Holy cow, what a ride!!!"

When I was a young housewife everything was an adventure for us. We were always on the edge of something exciting; at least we always thought so! We were ready to take over the world. We knew no bounds, we were sowing our wild oats.

We were the last generation where a mom could stay home to be a mom, guilt-free. I was the only mom who worked and I worked for my husband, so you didn't even get to count that as work . . . it was like a game. I worked when I wanted to and I was always ready and willing to give up on work to go looking for an adventure.

So, one day my friend Donna called and said, "Wanna ride to Berlin with me?" Great . . . an adventure! So, we packed up our babies and off we went. One very vital piece of information I give you about my

friendship with Donna is that she has no sense of direction. But as she had lived in Ripon all her life, it never occurred to me she would not find Berlin, Wisconsin, ten miles away.

But there we were, bouncing down the highway, laughing and chatting and catching up, our kids singing and playing in the backseat. All of a sudden Donna said, "Oh, we're in Rosendale . . . that's on the way to Fondy. Must be I have to go left." So, left we went. Nothing stopped us. Oops, then she was frowning again. No joy in Donnaville! She was muttering that we were in Pickett, which was on the way to Oshkosh. No, this was still not the way to Berlin.

By that time we were doubled over in laughter and decided we could not find our way out of a paper bag with a guide! Where did we turn? Which way would we go? Amid our giggles we remembered that we were in Pickett, the home of the quadruple-dip ice cream cone made with Ripon Creamery ice cream. Heaven on earth! Off we went to the Pickett filling station and we placed our orders. For less than $1.00 each we had one of the best times of our lives, and it has given us so much joy repeating the story for the past forty years.

Remember, life is not always about the destination. Have a joyful journey; you never know where life will take you. Sometimes it's just to Pickett, Wisconsin, for the best ice cream cone in the whole world.

20

Everything's Possible

Years ago I was at a party given by my friend Beth in Green Lake, Wisconsin, when I became aware of a guest who looked like she had stepped right out of the pages of *Vogue*. Although she was barely five feet tall, she could have given any supermodel a run for her money. Her dress was high fashion, her nails were beautifully manicured, and her shiny cropped blonde bob ended precisely at her chin. Every detail was perfect. She was so chic that it made my teeth hurt. During the party, we were all abuzz with speculation as to who she was. Most of us assumed that she was a tourist and outsider of the most despicable kind: You guessed it, she had to be one of those *Chicago* people.

The next weekend was my twentieth high school reunion. As I walked into the dinner that night, there she was again, the mystery woman. The next thing I knew she was walking up to me. As she said, "Hi, Jeanne!" I was frantically running through the names of the ninety people in my graduating class. I smiled and greeted her while casually glancing at her name tag for a clue to her identity. It said "Nancy Furr." My maiden name is Freund and because the nuns always sat us in alphabetical order, I would have remembered someone named Furr. As we talked, it suddenly came to me. This was Nancy Kohlman. I had known her all through school. She was always a fun and wholesome farm girl. I remembered her as the perky cheerleader, miles away from the fashion plate with the husky voice that stood in front of me.

I could see, the more we talked, that she was everything I remembered and more. She was still great fun, but she had added a sophistication and polish that was exciting to be around. I learned that she had become a well-known designer and had married a jet-setting executive of a popular ad agency. That day we both learned the joy of rediscovering old friends and making them into new friends.

I still talk to Nancy at least once a month. She is a walking testimony to the power of someone to make herself over into the person she always longed to be. I only have to think of her to remember that everything is possible when you set your mind to it.

Today I Wish Upon You Ordinary Miracles . . .

A call from an old friend
A great parking spot
when you go shopping
The fastest line in the grocery store
Green lights all day
Your favorite '50s song on the radio
to sing along with
A day of peace . . . happiness and joy

Listen to Your Heart

Call it heart, call it intuition, call it God.
All I know is when I become quiet
(and you know that's hard for me)
and I listen to my inner voice,
things begin to happen.

Listen to your heart
and watch your dreams come true!

21

What Do Rich Women Do?

People always ask how I got to be a business woman . . .

Well, I was a very happy, rich wife. I shopped, entertained, played, and did it all very well. This was not really fulfilling, however, so I began to study my options by studying women who had gone before me. This was the list I came up with:

. . . I could continue to be bored, or

. . . I could drink, or

. . . I could do charity work, or

. . . I could have an affair, or

. . . I could kill my husband, or

. . . I could have more kids and kill me, or

. . . I could go to work.

And that's just what I did. Actually, I went shouting and screaming into a job, but it was my only option. I had done all the good stuff on my list, and my dad's face came to mind every time I thought about doing the

bad stuff. Although truth be told, drinking and [h]an affair did appeal to me!

I believe we have a plan for our life built i[n] when we are born. Look how mine came about. [ ] is yours? Have you found it yet?

Mine was way down in the very pit of my st[ ] Where are you keeping yours?

22

Just Another Perfect Day

The summer before my freshman year of college, I met the perfect husband candidate: Arlow Bice Jr. This man, to me, was marriage material and I loved him very much. I was very lucky; he felt the same about me. It's funny how life works out. I had been working on my MRS degree (as we called it in those days) and after graduation we got married. I loved being married. I believed it was what God created me for. I could be the nurturer, the nester, and Mother Earth all wrapped into one. I loved my home and family more than words could say. I really did have a perfect life, a wonderful life—perfect children and a big house to play in and decorate and entertain. I could do just about anything I set my mind to. I was the princess of everything.

We got married in 1959, a perfect time to be alive. You knew your life would be better than your parents', and you just knew you would succeed. I think we were the last generation that was allowed to be fat or thin, to be pretty or ugly, geeky or a cheerleader. We were still a generation who got married first and *then* lived together.

We were the last generation so dumb to think you needed a husband to have a baby. Life was perfect, and I was perfect at it.

Butch was the perfect man for me. I could be center stage. I could look like I was running the show, but he was really the person in command. He would give me the love and the grace to be who I was and I could go on and do anything I wanted. Marriage was absolutely the perfect place for Jeanne Bice.

I was the me that God created me to be.

On March 31, 1981, it was just another perfect day in Jeanne Bice's perfect life. The tulips and the daffodils we had planted the previous fall were the biggest and the prettiest we had ever seen. Spring had come early to Wisconsin. It was almost downright hot outside. My husband and I sat in the kitchen having lunch, talking about how lucky we were and how great life was. If this day was any indication, it would be a perfect summer. Butch had stayed home from work that morning to clean up the winter debris from the backyard. The flowerbeds were beginning to stir and needed their blanket of leaves removed. He talked about calling the pool man . . . this was the earliest ever! We also talked about how we sat around all winter like slugs, and how the morning's yard work had really tired him out. Butch said that we should start a walking regime when he came home from work that evening. I promised to get home early so we could do it before dark.

After lunch, Butch went to the grocery store to pick

up a few things. When he had gone, Mary Ann, my business partner, came by to go over some last-minute details. She was on her way to an out-of-town funeral, and I would have to run the ship for a few days. We cleared up a few things, and she went back to the den to use the phone as Butch returned from the grocery store. We unpacked the groceries, and chatted about a few more things until he turned to me, gave me a kiss, and said, "I love you, Jeanne." He turned to go back to work and dropped dead at my feet, right there between the kitchen and the breezeway. When he hit the floor, he made a single, mournful noise.

You know, it's funny how life prepares you for times like this. The year I got married, my father-in-law became ill. He was the strongest man I had ever known in both body and spirit. All of a sudden, he was dying and they couldn't fix it. One day I was sitting with my sister-in-law in the sunroom of the hospital right outside his room. It was very early in the morning, and the nurse came in and told us that Mr. Bice had gone to Heaven and asked if anyone wanted to come in and say goodbye. My sister-in-law was too close to him and just couldn't do it. Well, I barely knew the man, so I said I would go in. I was very young and very naive.

I walked into the room and there he was. He was making this noise, like a loud engine running down. I turned to the nurse and told her that she had made a mistake and that Mr. Bice was still alive. She very sweetly told me, "No, my dear, it's just his motor shutting off." That sound haunted me for years. It was such a mournful sound. Well, as my dear, sweet Butch dropped to the floor, I heard that sound again. It was the same mournful sound and at that instant I knew that *my* Mr. Bice had gone to Heaven.

I stood for a moment and then screamed, "Mary Ann, come quick! Call for an ambulance! DO SOME-THING!" This was 1981 and the emergency 911 system was just being set up in our small town. I screamed, "Call 411 and get help!" She got information, who finally put her through to 911. I was only five off! Help was on the way, but I knew the life we had been living five minutes earlier was gone, gone for good.

The whole medical community was waiting for us at the hospital to save my Butchie. As I sat and waited for the doctor to tell me what I already knew, friends began to gather. They were there to hold out hope that it was not true. Finally, our dear friend and family doctor, Ted Ramos, came over. He squatted down in front of me and said, "Jeanne, Butch is gone." Then he turned to my friends Mary Ann and Donna and said, "There's something wrong here, she's not crying. She seems to be in a trance, almost at a loss for words." People who knew me knew that never happened with Jeanne.

Would you like to know what was going through my head? Silly things like, "Oh, my God, there goes my method of birth control. Oh, what will happen to a fat widow of forty? Things are not going to be like they used to be. What do I do?" Not the usual things that you'd think would have been going through my head—like what I would tell his family, how I would tell our precious children. Then I heard this voice. It was very strong, very loud, like it was right in the room with me. It said, "Okay, Jeanne Bice, now is the time for you to be the person I created you to be." It was time for me to finally grow up. I was in charge, like it or not.

They say that God never gives us more than we can handle. Right at that moment, I was quite sure God had really blown this one. There was no way I would make it through this. I felt I had been thrown into a very deep, dark pit and that there was no way out.

My friends kept saying that I was a strong person and that with their help we would all get through this. But I just could not and would not believe it.

Looking back on that time, I see this was a perfectly normal reaction. I also see that it was one of the first times that I experienced an important part of believing. Sometimes life is so hard it becomes difficult to believe that it can get better. It is at these times that we can fall back on friends and family and let them believe for us until we are strong enough to believe for ourselves.

There have been times in my life when I have hurt so bad. I just knew my heart had broken, but I had no clue how to deal with it. I thought I would never heal! If there was a hospital with a trauma center that could sew my heart back up, that's what I needed. Oh, what to do? "Poor me."

When I was a little girl, if my dolls had a broken

heart, leg, or arm, I fixed it with a kiss. Pure love fixed all injuries. Well, I've learned that pure love still fixes a broken heart. A warm smile is like a stitch or two and a big hug is just like the bandage. Love is a warmth that heals.

Where Faith Begins . . .
Worry Ends.

23

You Can Put Humpty Dumpty Back Together Again

After my husband died, I did feel just like Humpty Dumpty. Late at night I would lie in my king-sized bed alone, wondering who would put me back together again. For me, the answer wasn't found in a self-help book or in a new beau, it was in the arms of a small town.

Everyone seemed to be willing to offer me advice on how I could find the strength to go on. One of the best pieces of wisdom I followed was to accept every invitation that came my way. Soon my schedule was very full. It went something like this:

Wednesday night:

I had a standing invitation to Joan and Gordon Bischoff's for dinner. Joan is a wonderful cook and many a stuffed pork chop lessened my grief that year. Every week I would cry as I pulled out of their driveway. I always had the feeling that there was a tear in their eyes, too, for what had been.

Friday night:

Friday quickly became Fish Fry Night with the Longs, the Brauns, and the McMillans. Every week Jerry Long would pick us up in his current van. He was the local car dealer so his van was usually the size of a New York apartment and equipped with all the very latest gadgets. Everyone would pack in and off we went in search of the perfect fish fry. We would shake dice for drinks, laugh, talk loudly, overeat, and just enjoy one another's company.

Their greatest gift to me during those months was to talk about Butch naturally and without drama. To them I was still Jeanne and not the poor Bice widow. After the evening ended, Jerry would drive me to my door and watch to make sure I made it safely in. I would cry myself to sleep, but I knew I could make it through the week until Friday because they would once again be there for me.

WE TRANSPORT JOY!

SPECIALS

Saturday night:

Saturday night was dinner at a restaurant in Green Lake with the Furrs, the Talbergs, and the Beers if they were in town. Every week, I would drive the familiar road to Green Lake. For the next two and a half hours I would be wrapped in a mantle of joy and love. Just for a moment, life seemed to be back to normal.

Sunday:

Sunday after-
noons were reserved for
sitting by the pool with the
Rogerses. My daughter, Terry,
and Becky Rogers were friends from
school, but I had never really known
Tom and Jenny until Butch's funeral. They were
one of the many couples who brought a dish to pass and
stayed to become lifelong friends. Butch and I had
never socialized with them as couples so they weren't
part of my old life. Maybe that's why Sundays were so
special as we sat, soaked up the sun, and generally
recharged our batteries for the upcoming workweek.
Tom and Jenny were friends of Jeanne the single
woman, not of Jeanne the remains of a couple. I would
still go home and have a good cry, but I knew I had a
good reason to hang on for the weekend.

Angels come in many shapes and sizes. These friends
were truly angels on earth to the children and me. They
have certainly earned their wings, though their halos
might be slightly askew! I thank God for their friendship
during that first hideous year. I owe them my life.

Every journey through grief and into your new life
on the other side is a day-to-day struggle. In the comforting arms of a small town I found the strength to
hold on until that chain of days became months and the
desperation of my grief began to ebb.

24

My Miracles Come by Phone

There's one thing about death: It's so final. There's no, "Ooops . . . I just need to ask one more question." He was gone and there were no more questions. That was that.

I kept saying, "I think God needs to rework that one detail. I thought I should be given a couple of phone calls to have a good-bye . . . to find out where stuff is . . . just to hear his voice."

After Butch died, for the first time in my life, I had trouble sleeping. I would crawl out of bed and fall to my knees and beg for answers. "Oh please, God, let him call me." Finally, out of exhaustion, I would crawl back into bed and fall asleep.

About a week into this ritual, the phone rang at 2:00 a.m. I got up to answer it and I just knew it would be him. But no one was there. This happened night after night, week after week, for almost a month and a half. Slowly it began to comfort me. It almost said to me, "It's okay, Jeanne, you're going to make it. You've got the stuff . . . you'll figure it out. I'm watching over you, Jeanne."

When the middle-of-the-night mystery calls ended, it was a little like I had lost him again. But by then I had begun to see that I would make it on my own. God gave me that little extra bit of help I needed in the form of a phone call.

A phone call can be the beginning of many great changes.

A little more than a decade ago I got a phone call from the State of Florida to see if I would like to try out for QVC' s 50-50 tour. That phone call started me on a remarkable journey that has brought me more joy and excitement than I can say. It also led to more calls.

When we succeeded on the 50-50 tour audition stop in Florida and went to our first meeting at QVC, we were shown to a small conference room where we set up our rack full of samples. We were excitedly preparing to do our thing for a group of three or four buyers, when, out of nowhere, a whirlwind of energy came flying into the room in the form of an excited young woman. She started asking, "Where have these people been? They were supposed to be back on the air a month ago!" Then she walked over to the rack and said, "Oh my God, we've got to buy this and this and this."

This was Susan Bramley, and she was our "planner."

We came to learn that the planner works together with the buyer to pick when and what kind of product goes on the air for sale. Susan was a very good planner and a strong supporter of the Quacker Factory line for six years.

> *Miracles happen between people all the time.*

One day I got a phone call from Susan and she said, "Jeanne, I had a dream last night. It said to start my own consulting business and ask Quacker Factory to be my first client. Take the risk, leave my job, and together we'll be great. I'm going to do it. Will you be my first client?" I looked to the heavens and said, "Thank you, God!" A phone miracle.

Years ago I asked my dear friend John Furr how I could get on the *Oprah Winfrey Show*. John is an executive vice president in the Chicago offices of J. Walter Thompson, an international advertising agency. He is a marketing guru, and he said, "Jeanne, write a book, then go to Oprah." A good idea, and ten years later here we are.

Since that conversation I would always kid with him that if he was ever ready for a change, he could come work with the Quacker Factory! One day the phone rang when I least expected it. "Hi, this is John.

How would you like a new consultant?" I again looked to the heavens and said, "Thank you, God!" Another phone miracle.

During the time I had been writing the book we always thought we would have to self-publish. We went to publishers and tried to cut deals, but they were never just right. In the end, I thought, I had waited this long, the right person will just come to us and it will be great.

One evening I had just sat down to relax after a very busy day, and the phone rang. I was so tired, I just couldn't face another call, but something inside me said, "Pick it up, Jeanne . . . this one's good." I answered the phone, and this sweet voice, out of the blue said, "I understand you've got a book. I want to publish it." And, I looked to the heavens and said, "Thank you, God!" Another phone miracle!

I could go on and on with many stories, but I think you can see miracles come in many ways. Mine come by phone. Open your arms up, let them fly into you.

25

Suck It Up & Handle It!

Take sadness, take tragedy, take the horrible thing, the thing that would break most people . . . and take it to greatness.

Shortly after Butch died, my daughter, Terry, came into my bedroom, riddled with tears. This was so hard for her. She was daddy's little girl and had been very spoiled, very much the little princess. She went off to school one morning a happy teenager with the perfect life—a mom, a dad, and a big brother. She came home to "No Dad." There was no sickness, no good-bye, no preparation.

We had cried, we had mourned, we had cuddled, and we had loved. In my weakened state, I even tried to make it all better by letting her have her ears pierced. Her dad always said that no one in our family would ever have their ears pierced, that it was "a gross mutilation of the human body." Well, I always thought that was so stupid, but in a family you pick your battles and this one had not been worth fighting. Besides, in my head only biker babes or people who hung out with the wrong crowd ever had their ears pierced (or wore ankle bracelets). Same trampy stuff. So for years, I had sided with her dad.

But now, I had to pull a magic rabbit out of the hat, and I used the pierced-ear card. But even this did not bring joy to our sad home. As she crawled into my bed one night, she moaned, "Oh, Mom, I just came from the cemetery. I want to die. I don't want to go on."

Oh, dear, sweet God, I thought, what do I do now?

I turned to her and said, "Honey, you have two choices . . . you can lay down in the cemetery and die, or you can get up out of this bed and go on to live a life that will honor your father. Make him proud he had you for a daughter." She looked at me with both shock and hate in her eyes, and hissed "You bitch!" at me and stormed out of the room. At that moment I knew she was going to be okay. She had her fight back. Since then she has indeed taken her life to glory for her dad.

So often I say to my kids, "Oh, if only your dad was here to see what you have accomplished." We, as a family, have banded together. We have accomplished things in our lives that could never have been done before. Butch's father was enormously successful, a very strong, aggressive figure who ran his world with a firm, iron hand. Butch always said that he could never be as good as his father . . . that he could never live up to him. But what he *could* do was raise a family with strong ideals, great morals, and true hearts. This he has done. He raised all three of us to be our own individuals. I watch

Faith
makes things possible,
not easy . . .

my son cut deal after deal to give us financial security, to protect us from ever being in want again. I've watched him give up his dreams so I could live mine. I watch as he carries all the stress of this business, so Terry and I can create our dreams. What a gift he has given us.

One of the things my kids say is that they never got to know their dad as a friend. He was still just Dad. My children and I have become best of friends as we've grown older. We have fun as equals . . . we're partners. They didn't get to do this with their dad. Oh, but what they have done is given his life a purpose. It's why he was born. Having this family was what he was born to do. They've done him proud and they've taken me along for the ride.

Yes, bad things do happen to good people. And when they do, we tend to get angry. I came to realize that not only do we have to forgive others and ourselves, sometimes we even need to forgive God. His vision for us is so much greater than our own that we often mistake His plan as being wrong. Being mad at God is part of our humanness. Being able to forgive Him makes us divine.

26

I Give Up!!

What changes our lives? There are all the big things like marriage, new baby, deaths, and, of course, winning the lottery!

But what about the little things that come into our lives just for a fleeting moment, like a great teacher in second grade, a nice lady sitting next to you on a plane, the kid who delivers the pizza and is extra sweet, or the cute guy that winks at you in the check-out line at the grocery store?

Each one of these events and people leaves a mark on our lives. Some leave us a thought that changes our lives. Pastor Ron Dingle from Advent Lutheran Church in Boca Raton, Florida, was one of these people.

In the early eighties, as a raw, new widow, I moved to Boca Raton to open a new retail store and I was looking for a Florida church. The woman who was managing the store asked me what my affiliation was. When I told her, she said that her son-in-law was the assistant pastor at a Lutheran church in the area. Since this is what I was shopping for, I tried it. It was run by Pastor Dingle and Assistant Pastor Dangerfield.

Now, you've got to love a church headed up by Dingle and Dangerfield. It sort of sounds like a Vegas act. I knew it was going to be a special place.

And that it was. The first Sunday I walked in, I received a wonderful, friendly welcome from the greeters. I sat down in a pew next to a great, older couple who spent some time inquiring how my world was. They truly cared.

As the service proceeded, I had a great feeling of love. It just washed over me. As we sat down to hear the sermon, men put their arms around their families. Friends moved closer to friends, and children crawled into their grandmas' laps. Everyone's attention was glued to the pastor's words. This man had a way of holding you in the palm of his hand and never letting you go.

The sermon and feeling it left inside me is as fresh in my mind today as it was on that day in October of 1981.

The sermon was on "Running Your Life." It included the good stuff, the bad stuff, and how to handle it all. He had an answer. I, for one, needed answers in my world. I settled in, waiting for the magic potion he was giving out.

He simply stood before us that day and said, "When life gets to be too much to handle, just give it over to God." That's it. That's one of those sentences that ultimately changed me, and the way I do things. Pastor Dingle said, "God is waiting for us to give up control and let Him do it." They were the simplest words to hear and the hardest words I have ever tried to live by.

You see; I would give my troubled life over to Him real easy. But then, I would rush to grab it back. Sometimes in minutes, sometimes in hours; I never lasted a whole day without trying to take back control. I am definitely a control freak.

For the next fifteen years, I struggled through great ups and downs—my pains and pleasures, my sadness and joys. I was always trying to get my life under control and I was failing at it miserably. My brother was paying my expenses; my friends were giving me money. I was, as they say, between the ol' rock and a hard place. My business and personal lives had gotten so bad and the money was so tight that I was afraid I could literally end up a homeless person with a grocery cart living under the Oakland Park Boulevard Bridge.

My son, Tim, who had also become my business partner by this time, said, "Mom, the way you're running your life just isn't working and you always talk about that Dingle sermon. Why don't we try giving it up to God and leaving it in His hands this time."

I told him that would do no good because I couldn't just sit around on my fat ass and expect God to do it all. But my son believed that we could do just that. He asked me, "If there was one thing you could do different, Mom, what would it be?"

I said, "Funny you should ask."

My cable television had just gotten a new station called QVC. It was TV shopping, and the more I watched it the more I believed it was what God had created me for.

So, that day, I put a huge sign on my office wall that said "QVC YES!!" I sat down and said, "God, it's in your hands—I am open to your miracles! I am giving my life over to you—do with me as you choose."

For the next two days I had the worst case of the hives I have ever had in my entire life. I was scared to death. This giving up control was not all it was cracked up to be. What if God wanted me to go to India to feed the poor? I really, really, really did not want to do that. On day three, after going through an entire case of calamine lotion, I called a friend to discuss my fears. She calmly explained that firstly, God didn't need me in India since Mother Theresa had that covered. Secondly, God created Jeanne with certain talents. She told me that if I kept the faith and let Him use me and my talents, I would be amazed at the life I would have.

Two weeks later the chamber of commerce of the State of Florida called our office and asked if we had ever heard of QVC. I said yes! QVC YES!! YES, YES, YES!!!

They told us that QVC was having auditions for new products in all fifty states and asked if we would like to participate in the Florida call. Again I said yes.

Well, we passed the audition. Now we have one of

the most successful product lines on the network. And not only that, my personal life has been richly blessed in ways I could never have imagined. The people I have met and the stories I have heard fill me daily with more joy and love than I would have thought to ask for.

The first step toward getting somewhere is to decide that you're not going to stay where you are, that there are no real barriers to your success. You need to give up doubt and believe in possibilities . . . you can be who you want to be with a little help from a good friend . . . God. We don't need an explanation for everything. There *are* miracles in this life. When you believe something great will happen, it will happen. This is the key! The dreams you believe in can come true. Set your goals high. If you begin with wild expectations, you will succeed beyond your wildest expectations. Remember, in the words of Pastor Dingle, "Give it to God"!

Hanging on to resentment is letting somone you despise live rent-free in your head.

Write It on a Post-it Note and. . .

PUT IT ON THE WALL . . .

PUT IT ON THE REARVIEW MIRROR

PUT IT ON THE FRIDGE

PUT IT ON THE BEDPOST

PUT IT ON THE DOG'S TAIL

PUT IT ON THE END OF YOUR NOSE

STAY FOCUSED!!!!!

27

Forgive & Forget

To err is human, to forgive is divine.

I have found that there is nothing in life that blocks the flow of God's blessings like a wrong that has been done us that we have left unforgiven.

My husband used to say that I was very quick to forgive but I would never, ever forget. I was a world-class grudge holder. I have come to learn that holding a grudge is not only a waste of time but takes up an extreme amount of energy. Energy that could be better spent dreaming, believing, and being grateful.

Ultimately, forgiving means letting go. As the old saying goes—forgive and forget. This was a very difficult concept for me to get my arms around. I didn't even want to grasp it because I was so wrapped up in the anger I felt over what some people had done to me.

Throughout the years I had a variation of the same scenario happen to me over and over again. I would hire a person to work for me, I would train them in my craft, and they would, through my business, make a good living. After a year or two they would start to feel that they had the whole thing figured out and I would find that they were stealing my ideas and goods and selling them out the back door. I would fire them and the hurt and anger would hang in my soul like a gloomy cloud for months.

Then came the old straw that broke the camel's back. After I moved to Florida and before I got on QVC, I sold clothes at flea markets up and down the East Coast. There was a young couple I worked next to one flea market who were having a rough time of it financially. I needed some help keeping up with making my hand-painted clothes, so I hired them, trained them, and gave them a trade. For years they worked for me and I really thought I had found that rare animal in today's world—the trustworthy employee. I was wrong. One day I found them doing the same thing all the others before them had right at the same flea market where I had found them years before.

I began to study forgiveness. The anger and hate were driving me crazy. Hating partners who had screwed me, hating employees who screwed me, and hating old boyfriends who had screwed me! All this hate seemed to just be screwing me up. I needed it to end, I needed to forgive. But how?

I asked for help and this is what I found. A friend suggested that every time I felt the hate and anger come up toward a person, to say the following:

Dear God,

    I ask them to forgive me for any hurt I may have caused them in their life. I forgive them for all the hurt they have caused in my life. I give it all to you, God. I release it. I let it go.

In the beginning I had days where repeating this was all I had time to do. But over time it worked. The anger is gone. Now whenever I am hurt I use this prayer and the anger never has a chance to fill my life. I can better use that energy elsewhere. I also like to use it on myself, because sometimes I don't forgive *me*, either.

    Try it yourself. Go ahead, forgive and forget. Clear that road and get ready to receive the blessings that life has in store for you.

28

A Pot to Piss In, a Window to Throw It Out

I got to a point in my life where I was very close to living under a bridge with a grocery cart, a true bag lady. I had very little money. I was at the flea market selling the few clothes a week I could hand paint myself. I would paint the front of the garments during the day, and then at 1:00 a.m., when they were dry, I would flip them and paint the backs. I was working eighteen to nineteen hours a day and hardly hanging on. My brother was paying my rent. Was this the way it was going to end? The people kept saying, "Jeanne, go get a job where you get a paycheck, benefits, and you know what's coming in each week. Just give it up!" What they didn't realize was that I wasn't hanging on to my own business out of stubbornness, I was hanging on because I had no other place to go. I was between that ol' rock and a hard place. I was in my fifties, overweight, never had a real job in my life. Who was ever going to hire me? What could an old woman bring to any company? So I just kept doing what I had been doing and hoped life would get better.

In the middle of the night, I would have these flashbacks. My mother was the queen of having lunch in big department store dining rooms, or at the lunch counters of dime stores and drugstores. She just loved to go out to lunch, and these were places that a woman could eat alone and it was considered proper. Every table or counter stool was filled with women eating alone. Often I got to go along with her and I loved it. Hey. It was a *food* outing. As a young child I always noticed that the waitresses were older than God, and I would ask my mom why they were still working. Conversations about retirement were big in my house. My dad's goal was to retire at fifty and have enough money set aside to support them the rest of their lives. He talked about it every day, so I figured everyone retired at fifty. But here were women in their seventies and eighties, still shuffling along and slinging hash with a pretty hanky in their pocket. My mom's answer was always the same: "They work because they don't have a pot to piss in or a window to throw it out, Jeanne. Save your money, girl, or this will be you someday."

As I lay awake worrying night after night, bills piling up in the basket by the front door not even opened, phone turned off until I got to the Sears store to have it turned back on, I realized I could be one of those ladies with not a pot to piss in or a window to throw it out. I saw this as a trial, and it was happening to me.

Suppose you go to a friend's house and she serves the absolute most wonderfully delicious cookie you have ever tasted in your whole life, and you beg for her special recipe, and then after promising to babysit her kids for a month and to vacuum her lawn and dust her house, she gives it to you? You are so thrilled that you rush home to make this perfect morsel. But, oops, it's not the same. Then you try again. Nope, not the same. So, you try one more time, and another failure. At this point, you tell yourself to get a grip and look for a new recipe. You don't just continue to bake bad cookies. It's a waste of time and a waste of cookie money.

But in those years I was running my life that same way, even though it wasn't working. There is always another choice!

We don't always have to shop at the same store. We don't have to work at any particular job. We don't have to stay in any given relationship.

We can choose. We can decide to change the course of our lives at any time. We have the power and no one can take it away from us.

So there I was, continuing to live my life the same way and creating the same result . . . failure. I needed a new cookie recipe. A new recipe on how to pull myself up by my bra straps and get on with my life. But this time I would make *success* the goal.

So, I set out on a crusade. I read books, I listened to tapes, and I studied Woo Woo things like yoga and meditation. The problem was that I couldn't shut up long enough to meditate and if by some chance I did succeed, I would fall asleep only to be awakened by my own loud snoring. The first time I did yoga I tied myself up in such a knot that I thought I would remain that way forever! Luckily someone came along and put me back on my feet.

I read that I needed to visualize what I wanted and it would come. But I could not envision success, all I could envision was my bills, my creditors calling, and all the people I had let down. So much for Woo Woo.

Then one day someone said to me, "Jeanne, just fake it till you make it." Well, it's hard to fake that you have a lot of money when they are taking away your car and turning off your phone. My friend said, "No, no, no, you can't fake it to the world, just fake it in your head." So, each day I would round up enough money—by pawning something or by finding change in the bottom of drawers and purses—to go out and pay a bill or to buy a few groceries. Do you know how shitty it is to pay your phone bill with quarters, dimes, nickels, and pennies? The whole world just knows that you don't have a pot to piss in, much less a window to throw it out.

So, instead of saying over and over in my head, "Oh, my God, I have no money, I'm broke, I'm going to die," I found a new mantra, a *new recipe*. I would say this one thing in my head over and over and over again: "Thank you, God, I have more money than I will ever be able to spend. Thank you, God, I have more money than I will ever to be able to spend." I would repeat it in the line at Sears instead of being embarrassed that I had to be there; I would repeat it in my head at Publix while paying for groceries; I would repeat it over and over whenever I had anything to do with money. "Thank you, God, I have more money than I will ever be able to spend."

And now, years later, I do. I believed it would work, and it did.

I have a pot . . . one that stands a little higher than the rest of them so I don't have to go down so far! And I also have beautiful windows to throw it out. "Thank you, God. I have more money than I will ever need. Thanks lots!"

Checkbook Prayer

I keep this prayer in my checkbook so that when I write a check I am reminded that in God's world there is abundance:

> "I write this check and I spend this money with gratitude for the abundance of God's goodness in my life today. With love I release it into the flow of life, knowing it goes forth and returns to multiply. Bless and prosper me and all those it touches."

29

Stop the Insanity!

Every year all the girls—Jane, Sherry, Patty and I—
gather for our annual "week to catch up" in Florida.
We've been doing this since the early 80's when we
needed each other to support our new lives.

Over the years, we have wallowed in our pain, gig-
gled about dating again, shared stories of new jobs, suc-
cesses and failures, and been just plain rowdy together.
It was one week a year we could be whatever we wanted
to be and no one cared or judged. We just laughed till
we wet our pants and then laughed some more. We
would gather to be silly and shop, and we never let each
other down.

Twenty-five years later, I find we still laugh a lot but
now we go to bed earlier and drink less and eat health-
ier. No one even smokes anymore! And now our major
topics are bad knees, husbands' retirements, and our
grandkids. Oh, where have the wild, wacky women
gone . . . the rowdy bunch? We became happy, settled,
sweet, old sexy women and we love it!

I want to share a granny story! Patty's little granddaughter Emma is about two and was feeling her oats one day. She told her mom she would sit in a big person's chair at dinner. "No booster seat for me, Mommy." Well her mom, Alissa, told her in a very stern, motherly voice, "No, you will do it my way and sit in the booster seat." She stood very still and did not say another word. So my friend Patty, the ever-helpful grandma, went to get the booster chair. As she carried it toward the table, Emma stood firm, feet planted squarely under her, put both of her hands up to Grandma, palms up and out and said in a very stern voice, "Stop, stop, stop!"

What a lesson she was to all of us. When things are going against what we believe, we need to say "STOP!" It's time to change. Out of the mouths of babes often comes the truth. Always remember, we can say "STOP!!" When life gets overwhelming and change becomes necessary, we can stop the insanity!

Now, poor Emma also learned a good lesson. She was still too young to have a mind of her own, and Mommy still knew best. She sat in that booster seat! But, my hope for her is she remembers that day and always keeps that spirit.

Let's all stand, plant our feet squarely under us, put our hands up, palms out and up, and shout, STOP! Oh, it feels so good. Go ahead, try it. No . . . Louder! LOUDER!

That's it, you've got it, kid . . . You can make a change any time. Just stand firm and shout STOP!

Be Inspired

I know that a "plan for your life" is harder to stick to than a diet! Life is unpredictable, often uncontrollable, and always full of gobs of surprises. Few of us wind up the person we set out to be!

I don't think any of us would have predicted a year ago that we would be doing the things we are doing today. Or that we'd be so happy with them. Especially since we seemed so happy a year ago doing what we were doing then, or so miserable we never thought we would feel joy again. Sometimes a year brings a big QUACK! QUACK! change, and sometimes a tiny peep! peep! change.

If you keep moving forward, adapting as you go, having faith, believing, you'll end up in a good place. If you need some motivation along the way, it's here for you. Take my hand, lean on me, cry with me. Let's get INSPIRED together!

The Lucky Ducky Stress Relief and Joyful Encounter Kit

The top-notch researchers that staff our high-tech lab at the Quacker Factory are involved in much more than the development of exciting new apparel for our loyal Quacker fans. They have a whole team devoted to putting more joy into life and getting all the stress out of it. These scientists have chosen as a model for this project the common duck.

The duck, as many of us know, has a distinct trait, which we humans would do well to emulate. Ducks move along the surface of a lake in a graceful and completely unruffled fashion. But under the surface of the water, they are indeed paddling like hell! Our research has shown that it is important to reach this stress-free state where everything you need to get done seems to happen by itself.

As a means to this end, our "Quack" scientists have developed a kit that will help to eliminate the stress from our lives so we can more effectively enjoy ourselves in all our pursuits. Use of the kit is simple. First, put on some relaxing music and start a hot bath. Introduce bubble bath into the tub. Float your rubber duck in this warm and lathery tub. Lastly, put a duck beak on your nose and climb in.

This will definitely put you in a "Quacky" state of mind, as you linger in a relaxing bubble bath surrounded by images of our friend the duck, from whom we've learned so much.

Additionally, when you go to your place of work, don't forget to bring your duck beak and whistle.* You will find these two items to be indispensable as those around you try to put stress into your life. There is absolutely no way anyone can mess with you when you're wearing a duck beak. Just in case someone tries, you can change his mind quickly with a few bleats on the whistle! This approach automatically guarantees a fun and stress-free encounter with anyone who comes your way.   —The Head Quack

Treat Yourself to a Lucky Ducky Kit!

Here's your list:

1. Bubbly bubble bath
2. Duck soap dispenser
3. A rubber ducky
4. Bars of ducky soap
5. A duck beak
6. A duck whistle
7. A small bottle of bubbles
8. Duck slippers
9. A ducky robe

Before you run screaming from your life, wondering just what the heck happened, go on and laugh. Laugh out loud. It'll do you good!

I'm too blessed to be stressed!

Always act like a duck . . . calm and unruffled on the surface, but paddlin' like hell underneath!

30

So What's the Next Dream?

God didn't create us to be "just so." He created us all with a dream. A heart's desire. When we were born we were filled with great possibilities. Creative thoughts and high dreams. And the talent to pull it all off. What we are to become in life is given to all of us at birth.

So often I say, "I was born to be a Rockefeller, but I came into life as a Freund." It's the truth. As my dad always said, "We are a Ford family, not a Cadillac family." For a long time I believed this was my lot in life. I was programmed to believe I could have the best Ford in town, but I couldn't get too big for my britches and try to go beyond that. These voices still run in my head now and then. But in my heart I also had a dream. I had my heart's desire. Yet if people asked me what my heart's desire was, I would say, "Just to have enough money to pay the phone bill on time." Just to keep this boat afloat, to hang on. And that was what I got. I was hanging on by the tips of my fake nails. I could always see myself living out of a grocery cart under the Oakland Park Boulevard Bridge in Fort Lauderdale. My heart's desire was staying one step ahead of that monster.

When my son first moved to New York many years ago, I told him to save his money or he'd be living on the street. As a joke, when he got there he told me he had found his first apartment. He said it was made out of the best corrugated cardboard box material. He sent samples of it to me. The wallpaper was newspaper, dishes were tin cans, heat was the air from vents in the road, and his food was from the best restaurant Dumpsters in town. It was a joke to show me he was okay, but there had been days when I thought this could be me. I was sure this is where I was heading if I didn't keep my nose to the grindstone and work hard.

When I learned more about getting my heart's desire I set my sights a bit higher and put that sign on my wall that said "QVC YES!" Then, as my confidence built, I began to realize that the sky's the limit. In fact, there's no limit at all. So I started dreaming bigger. Now you are reading my book: Another dream has come true.

I now have yet bigger dreams to dream. Recently we went into New York to meet with a press agent at a publicity firm we were thinking of hiring. We walked into this very chic office and saw that he had an impressive list of clients. He represented movie stars and had even worked for presidents. So I turned to him and said, "Ken Sunshine, why do you need me?" His response was, "You have a fire in your belly. You have a passion. It will be fun to watch you come into your own."

It was at this point that he turned to me and asked, "What do you *really* want to do? What is your dream? What is your heart's desire?" I sat there for a very long time, because I had never told anyone, except my kids, what that dream was. I kept it hidden under a bushel basket just like my dad told me to do. I just didn't know how to answer this question.

He turned to me and said, "You can dare to be happy with who you are right now and accept this as success, your success, and you would be just fine. But you came to me because you have a bigger dream. Whatever it is, let's work together with our whole heart and soul. Many people settle in life. I don't think that you were created to be happy halfway there. Let's go for the whole dream."

I finally decided, oh, hell, I don't know this man. I might not even see him again after I tell him this. E-gads, this is hard. How could a farm kid from Fond du Lac, Wisconsin, even have the nerve to spit this out? okay, here I go. I want to be a star. I want to have a television show. Somewhere between Mr. Food and Martha Stewart, somewhere between Ellen and Oprah, there is a place for me. A woman like every other woman, just doing stuff that women do. I could have Johnny Mathis and Martha over for lunch, and I could also have my very best friends on the show with me. All of the ones that are the best cooks, the best home designers, the best gardeners, the best social workers, and some that are just the best at being a best friend! I would do seasonal specials from my home, where I could have all my Quacker friends over and have fun and girl talk. I've learned this is what I do well, and this would give me more time to share my joy of life and have more fun.

So now it was out there. Ken's not rolling in the aisle, laughing at me, or calling me a big, fat dreamer. He looked me straight in the eye and said, "Let's go for it, Jeanne." I cried. He believed in me. Me, a nobody! He had a vision with me. Oh, I fell in love that day, and made a new friend.

This is my heart's desire. This is my passion. I love, love, love my day job and I would never give up QVC. I want it and everything else. QVC, a book, and to be a star with my own TV show. Maybe my family believed they were a Ford family. But maybe God wants me to live a Rolls-Royce life. I can't wait to see where we are going. I hope you'll come along for the ride.

Twelve Ways to Make Your Day More Quacky!

1. Wear your duck beak.
2. Take a bubble bath with your rubber duck.
3. Play a song on your happy duck whistle.
4. Do the ducky dance.
5. Waddle in joy; flap your wings.
6. Quack at everyone you meet.
7. Be the lead duck, fly upside down.
8. Play hooky from work when Jeanne is on QVC.
9. Go to lunch with friends and blow bubbles over martinis.
10. Catch a falling star and wear it on your toes.
11. Pick up a "man in the bar" and make it your husband.
12. Indulge in something sinfully delicious.

★   ★   ★

My brother always said, "If a deal sounds too good to be true, it is too good to be true. Walk away."

I look at my life now and it is too good to be true . . . and I'm keeping it! I love it and I deserve it. I am worthy of it!

Take the leap and grow wings on
your way down.

It's all there for the taking!

If I can do it, anyone can.

31

Unexpected Friend

My children mean more than anything to me, and it brings me great joy to know that they feel the same. This story was written to me some time ago by my daughter:

Friendship changes everything. Lonely? Get a friend. Sad beyond all endurance? Get a friend. Life to organize? Get a friend. I bet there isn't very much that you could think of, problem-wise, that couldn't be cured by the addition of a friend in your life.

Of course, the problem of where to find a friend springs to mind immediately. That may be the one problem that can't be cured by getting yourself a friend! But I also know that friends can be found in the most unusual and overlooked places.

How many people have met their very best friend at the grocery store, when they just ran in for a stick of butter? Or standing in line to buy concert tickets? Or maybe it was the cop who wrote their last speeding ticket? You may discover the best friend you could ever have is the neighbor you are sure is an ogre until the day he helps you take your sick child to the hospital when your car breaks down.

And, just possibly, horror of all horrors, you could find a great friend in your mother. I know what you're thinking, but the truth of the matter is that your mother was a person and a friend to other people long before she was your mother. It is within the realm of possibility that she could be a friend to you, too.

Of course this involves being old enough to realize that most of what she told you growing up was true. A hard lump to swallow, but once it's past your gullet, it can be as comforting as chicken soup. Then, if you can convince yourself not to let her push your buttons, you are raring to go.

It is really the best of the friendship world if you think about it. You already know her, so there is no awkward or embarrassing small talk to wade thorough. But you should spend lots of time talking to her because you'll learn the most amazing stuff. Like the kinds of things she did behind her mother's back, who she dated before your father, and which classes she flunked in school. Juicy stuff.

Also, she already has a built-in tendency toward doing things for you, and let's face it, who doesn't want that in a friend? Most of all, the love a mother bears her child is a love that can never be found in any other friendship, no matter where you search.

My daughter wrote this story to me during that unbelievably weird and wonderful time. That time in my life when my little baby was becoming an adult. As a parent I was selfish and sad to see her growing into an independent person; and yet, at the same time, as an adult she was giving me the gift of friendship, which turned out to be a blessing. To this day it fills my life in ways I can hardly understand.

Watch out for blessings. Someone you love is just itching to send one your way.

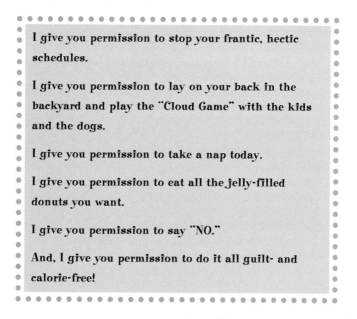

I give you permission to stop your frantic, hectic schedules.

I give you permission to lay on your back in the backyard and play the "Cloud Game" with the kids and the dogs.

I give you permission to take a nap today.

I give you permission to eat all the jelly-filled donuts you want.

I give you permission to say "NO."

And, I give you permission to do it all guilt- and calorie-free!

32

A Gal's Gotta Do What a Gal's Gotta Do

We all need some extra grit. We are all strong, wondrous people. Bravery, grit, guts, heart, nerve . . . and we all have it.

Mine sits at the very bottom of my stomach.

I spent my whole life acting like a wussy . . . I was just a little, weak woman. Now take a look at me. I'm big, I'm loud, and I'm raucous. There was nothing weak about me, except in my mind . . . in my head! But if I believed it, then I *was* weak, I kept this lie alive for years.

"What you believe is what you is." My greatest fear was that someone would discover I was a powerful woman.

Except God was watching. He had bigger plans for me, for my life! What does God have in mind for you? Listen, listen carefully . . . He's talking to you. What plans has He got for you? Let go, let them be!

33

I'm Not Perfect

"I'm not so thrilled with me. How could anyone else be thrilled with me . . . ?"

When I get these feelings about myself, I take a deep breath and try to remember a lesson I learned from my house the first time I saw it. It was not pretty. They called it the funeral home in the neighborhood. Yet I saw what it *could* be . . . I saw what just a little love could turn this house into.

It didn't happen overnight. I changed it bit by bit. I had a lot of help from friends and family, but when it was done a year later . . . oh, it was perfect! Or as close to perfect as I could conceive.

Yes, I made mistakes along the way. When I designed the new kitchen, I took down part of a wall to open it into the living room. Well, when they got it framed, I stood back and said, "Oops . . . I've made a big mistake, we've got to change it." The builder said we couldn't do it, that the cupboards would never fit if we did. But I knew it would be a bigger mistake if I didn't change it and would have to live with it the rest of my life. My challenge was to find a way for everything to fit and how to make the change at no extra cost. We all pulled together and made it work, and now it's perfect.

The last room I did was the room I was living in. By then, I was ready to be done with the remodeling thing. So, I did not take my time. I rushed. And when it was done, I hated the room. Now what should I do? Hey, this is not life and death. Change it . . . find creative ways to make it better.

One of the biggest mistakes we make in life is the "I made my bed, now I have to lie in it" kind of thinking. I can't tell you how many times I've heard my dad say that. Well, I've learned, we don't die if sometimes we have to remake that bed. And remake it I did. Now my living room is lovely! We get second, third, and fourth chances in life . . . when you make bad choices, just giggle and move on.

Each day I look around my perfect house and it reminds me of life. Today it's perfect. Tomorrow I will see a little paint is chipped, maybe a few lightbulbs are burnt out, there are ants in the cupboard, or the toilet will have overflowed. It doesn't mean the house is not perfect. It is just being what a house is.

It's our job to keep making life better. You know, you go along and you think, "Oh, hey . . . life is perfect," and then you begin to wonder, "When is the other shoe going to drop?" I'm not sure when the first shoe dropped, or even what a shoe dropping does. But my dad used to worry us with those shoes all of the time. So when it drops, what do we do? Crumble? Give up? Cry over spilled milk?

No, it's time to pull ourselves up by our bra straps and plunge back in. Get that house, our lives, or our thoughts back to perfect again!

34

The Two Questions

There are two questions everyone asks when they meet me: How did I get the name for the Quacker Factory, and why do I wear a headband? Well, these are easy!

My first business was a retail shop called The Silent Woman. Now, people who know me have a lot of trouble believing Jeanne Bice even knows what a silent woman is! We chose that name because we know the one time a woman is quiet is when she is shopping. We used the old headless-woman tavern sign from Civil War times as our logo. We just loved the humor of it because, in all reality, a woman is never silent.

When I moved to Florida we created a new label for the venture. It was called JB Duckworth. I chose this from a street sign in Connecticut. I thought "Duckworth" sounded very fancy-schmancy, and loved that it had "worth" in the name because our designs were "worth" it. We started our own factory with many, many, many women sewing for us.

One day I said to my son, "Oh, this is so much work. Just being in charge of all these women I never have time to do what I do best . . . create new ideas. All of this is driving me quackers! I bet I could rename this company 'A Quacker Factory' and take the clothes to the street corner and make more money with less work. Get the joy back in my life."

His answer was, "Then do it, let's go!" So, I was off to flea markets across the country. I loved it. I met wonderful women and learned a great deal about my craft. We have been quacking ever since! We really found ourselves in the world of Quackers.

What Makes a Woman Quack in Broad Daylight?

1. She has joy in her heart and a spring in her step.
2. She's looking for new friends.
3. She wants to strut her stuff.
4. She wants to wiggle her tail feathers.
5. She wants stand out among the crowd.

Now, why do I wear a headband? When I moved to Florida my very fine hair took a beating. I looked like a drowned rat who put her finger in an electrical outlet. It was not a pretty sight . . . almost downright scary! One day my daughter got tired of my bitching and suggested I do what every teenager at that time did when they had a bad hair day: tie a bandana headband around my forehead. "It will hold the hair up and back, Mom. Use your head!"

So, I had her whip one up for me, and off I went into the world. I was a new widow and now I had a new look! Over the last twenty-five years I have had many reasons to keep the headband:

First—it does keep the hair under control.

Second—I put it on and then pull all of the wrinkles up. Instant face-lift! I'm sure I look thirty-five years old.

Third—For many years I had a great business partner who I loved like a sister and who completed me. I was the sweet one and she was the bitchy one. Every good business needs both. Well, when people would call they always wanted to talk to me. My partner was stunningly gorgeous at 5'9", with long black hair. I was short and fat. That was how they asked to talk to me: "I want to talk to the short, chubby one." Well, once I started wearing the headband, they had a new way to identify me. They were much more comfortable asking for the partner with the headband.

I've saved the bestest reason till last.

Now when I'm out and about, all my wonderful

Quackers have a way of knowing it's me. They walk up to me, pointing to their forehead, saying, "It's you, isn't it?" Then they add a quick "Quack, quack!" Then we all giggle a lot together. I've met hundreds of people because of my headband.

I love it. No, I do not have a built-in ridge after all these years. But has become my trademark. It's always a good idea to keep your head above the crowd.

Reach for the Stars

This is my wish for you . . .

Smiles when sadness fills you
Laughter with lots of friends
Courage to like yourself
Faith to believe in the real you
Sunshine after the rain
Angels to carry you by your bra straps
while you reach for the stars!

It's very special!

35

We Create Our Tomorrows by What We Dream Today

DREAM LARGE.

"Just ask and it will come." When I say this to people I often hear, "Oh, I never get what I want," or "I'm just not lucky," or "I'm a *bad* magnet."

Ooops, listen to what's coming out of your mouth! With that attitude, if I were the "make-a-wish-come-true fairy," I'd fly right over your house, too. I know you wanted a bright red wagon or a big baby doll when you were little and you wished and wished and even wrote Santa Claus at the North Pole and never got it. You even bargained, you promised that if you got it you'd be nice to your brother for a whole year, and you still didn't get it.

My question is, Did you really believe you were going to receive it? Or, even as a child did you believe, I'm just not the lucky one?

You know, it really is simple for us to have our dreams come true. Just believe that they will, and ask. Let God deal with the details.

I was looking for a new condominium in 1991 and I

wanted it to be just perfect. I envisioned a very bright and airy home on the west side of the Intercoastal Waterway with large rooms, a great view, and a huge bedroom. One day I went on a showing and the moment I walked into the apartment, I knew it was mine. It was a corner unit with glass on two sides and I thought, "Oh this is great." The view took your breath away. This was exactly what I had asked for. I moved in believing I was the luckiest woman alive.

> *Dreams do have wings.*
> *Let them fly into your life——with an "I can do" attitude.*

However, this condo turned out to be a lesson for me. You see, I got the condo I asked for, but I forgot to ask for big closets and a big bathrooms! And there was only a teensy-weensy galley kitchen, which made it very difficult to entertain friends and family. So although I got what I dreamed of, I found out there was even more to come.

Dream Large!

God's plan for us is filled with abundance and I have learned to leave the details to Him. Sometimes we ask God for a Volkswagen and He has a Rolls-Royce in mind for us. If we are willing to settle, we may get something that was not intended for us. I learned that we are more open to receiving when we let go of control.

Dream of the little red wagon and let God create the best one for you. Then believe with your whole heart.

After a life of struggles this is one lesson I've learned. I have figured out when I sit back and look at my life as it is today, I would never have had the nerve to ask for all that I have received.

And all I had to do was . . .

DREAM LARGE!

Dream

Dream Big

Dream Very Big

Dream Very Very

Big!

Thank You!

Sometimes in the process of growing older and wiser, certain memories remain fresh in our minds. It has been so much fun sharing the memories that created the "Jeanne" that I am today. It is my hope that you have enjoyed this fun trip down memory lane, that it has brought you a giggle or two and perhaps an occasional tear.

It's hard to believe it has been ten years since I took a chance on my dream—since I made a promise to myself to give over the details of life to God. I've come so far and accomplished so much since then. Just think how much we have to look forward to! Every day I thank God for it all.

As the days and years keep coming, I wonder what the world has in store for me. My job now is to embrace new ideas with enthusiasm. Now I dream it, decorate it, and everything happens just the way it's supposed to. It all became so simple once I figured out the recipe! I would like to share it with you here:

Dream

Be Clear	Be Courageous
Be Creative	Be Thankful
Be Optimistic	Be Happy
Be Forgiving	Be Passionate
Be Giving	

Be Clear

Get a clear vision of your dream. What is your passion? Say no to what you don't want, and yes to what you do want.

Be Creative

Put your passion on the wall, on the bathroom mirror, on the dashboard, on the dog's nose. Just get it out there! Walk with purpose. Let it be easy!

Be Optimistic

Expect miracles. Open your arms and let them in—go for the magic! Give your dream wings.

Be Forgiving

Forgive yourself! Take responsibility for the good and bad. Failure is one of life's teachers. Celebrate it. Let go of the anger inside of you. Sweep out the fear. Forgiveness is a choice. Find strength in your failures. Adversity pushes us to our destiny, and we get many chances for do-overs in life.

Be Giving

We are not in this alone. Give, give, give from the heart. When your dream comes, share the ride with others.

Be Courageous

Give it up to a higher source. Let go, let God. He has great things in store for you. I received so much more than I ever had the guts to ask for. Faith is never knowing where we're going or how we're getting there, but loving the ride nevertheless. Follow the leader. If you fail, pull yourself up by your bra straps and try again.

Be Thankful

In everything, give thanks. Don't ever take life for granted. Be grateful for everything that happens in life, even your failures. It's so simple. Just say "thank you" and say it often.

Be Happy

Choose to be happy. Happiness is a decision you make, not an emotion you feel. Always find the joy in the day. What comes out of our mouths is what we live. Nobody's perfect; enjoy who you are!

Be Passionate

Keep walking toward your dream, feeling the passion in your belly. Life does get better than this. What you think in your head is what you get. Think success!

What *you* think is more important than what others think.

But most of all, *believe!*

Live bold and stand out in a crowd. Remember, fairy tales do come true.

Thanks for the memories!

Acknowledgments

My son got married ten years ago—July 2, 1995—and our first on-air at the QVC studio took place on July 3 and 4. My daughter, Lee, and I had to leave the fun wedding party to get on a plane to fly to West Chester, Pennsylvania. On the plane I said to Lee, "I have the greatest feeling this is going to be the ride of our life. And I'm not talking about the plane. I'm talking about this QVC thing. I think I should start writing a book." Being used to my harebrained schemes, Lee just looked at me and said, "Go for it, Mom."

Well it's been one hell of a ride. I want to thank all who have been with me on this roller coaster of a life:

To my kids, Tim and Lee, for living my dream.

To my brother and sister-in-law: who loved me enough to pay my way for over a year, and not tell me that I was crazy; and for enjoying my success.

Thank you, God, for a great family.

To my son-in-law, Mikey: With his heart he believed in me and supported me. He's our angel.

To my daughter-in-law, Karin, whose gut instincts have helped me stay out of trouble.

To the whole damn Graham family: You came with money and talent. You've done everything from making button covers to bagging and shipping. You took us shouting and singing into success and you brought along your friends. Let it snow, let it snow.

Susan Bramley: You are the wind beneath my wings. You've shown me how high I can fly.

John Furr: You said, "Write a book." It took a very long time, but here we are. You planted the seed, and you're a great gardener.

QVC: You gave me the showcase I needed to put my mouth into action. It's such an experience being a part of your family.

Lori and Kate: You make me look great and keep my chaotic life running smoothly. Hard job!

Tiago: You came to help and have stayed as part of our family. We all love you.

Pastor Ron Dingle: For my belief.

To all who have lived my life with me, thanks for being a part of my story. I hope you enjoy how you fit into the puzzle. You are all such good friends. And for those who didn't make this one; beware, there will be others.

To my mom and dad: for all your words that live in my head.

To my Butchie: You taught me to fly and loved me even when I "Quacked up."

To my Quackers: What a blessing you are in my life! Without you there would not be a Quacker Factory.

For Kelly and everyone at Hyperion, as well as Heather and Ken at Sunshine Consultants: Thanks for believing with me. You are Dream Makers.

To everyone who believed in my dream, that is what faith is all about. You could see the start, you didn't know where it was going, but you had enough faith in me to stick around. I hope you've enjoyed the ride as much as I have!